AF553598

THE CHAOTIC ORDER

THE CHAOTIC ORDER

An Unknown Teacher's Pedagogic Travelogue

Avijit Pathak

THE CHAOTIC ORDER: An Unknown Teacher's Pedagogic Travelogue
Avijit Pathak

© Author

First Published 2015

ISBN 978-93-5002-349-5 (Hb)

All rights reserved. No part of this book may be reproduced
or transmitted, in any form or by any means,
without the prior permission of the Publisher.

Published by
AAKAR BOOKS
28 E Pocket IV, Mayur Vihar Phase I, Delhi 110 091
Phone : 011 2279 5505 Telefax : 011 2279 5641
aakarbooks@gmail.com; www.aakarbooks.com

Printed at
Sapra Brothers, Delhi 92

To my daughter who, I believe, has realized that her father is primarily a child trying to be a teacher.

Preface

Here is a book on education, on pedagogy, on teaching, and on the ethos of the university as a centre for higher learning. But then, it is not like what professional sociologists of education would like to regard as an appropriate 'text' with theoretical as well as empirical chapters, with references and bibliography. In fact, here is a book which has no chapter in its standardized format; there is no structural design; instead, there are twenty reflexive narratives—not necessarily always arranged in a chronological order—through which I have sought to communicate with my readers. And the language I have used is not of the kind professional journals adhere to; instead, it flows like a river with its metaphors, symbols and poetic imagination.

In a way, the book is about what I do. I am a university professor. And as a researcher (yes, research is an integral part of the university life) I am expected to write on a spectrum of issues: modernity, culture, religion, politics, nationalism, globalization, ethnicity and identity. It is not that I escape from these professional obligations. However, I am also a teacher. And this aspect of my role in the university is no less important. In fact, it gives a distinctive identity to us; we are not just researchers; we are engaged in an act of communion with young learners. Have I ever bothered to reflect on what I do every morning as I enter the university—the practice of teaching, my engagement with my students, my pedagogic experiments? Is it possible for me to see my own practice as a text, read it, reflect on it, and write about it? In this book I have tried to do so; I have allowed myself to be contemplative and inner-directed; I have reflected on my own journey—what it means to exist primarily and fundamentally as a teacher, what it means to grow with students, and what it means to experiment, and rethink the very meaning of the university as a centre for higher learning.

A book of this kind, needlessly to add, cannot claim 'objectivity'. Because it is about my experience; it is about my context—my location in a leading central university that is not yet indifferent to the possibility of creative exploration; it is about my journey—my modes of learning and unlearning, my success and failure. Yet, the fact that I have chosen to publish it indicates that even though its fragrance is biographical, it has a story to tell that is likely to excite all those who reflect on education and pedagogy, the vocation of teaching, its deeper meanings, and the ethos of the university. It is not an egotistic venture (if my readers find the trace of my 'ego' in the text, I would consider it as my failure); it is all about connectivity and shared concerns.

Here is a book that emerges out of love and trust. My students have loved me. They have enabled me to evolve as a teacher, and reaffirm my conviction that to teach—and teach in silence—is an immensely graceful act. My protectors—my parents and my wife who have been constantly looking at me from the mysterious stars; my sisters and brothers; my loved ones; and above all, my daughter: I am eternally indebted to all of them. I trust Mr. Saxena—my publisher. I am grateful to him. And how elevated I would feel if my readers find a meaning in an unknown teacher's pedagogic travelogue, in this chaotic order!

Jawaharlal Nehru University
New Delhi
May 4, 2015

Avijit Pathak

1

I look at them. They surprise me. Even an examination, far from being oppressive, can be a celebration. My mind is filled with joy. I get my reward.

How elevated I feel as I narrate this incident! I have just come out from the examination hall. My students are writing their end semester examination. Some senior students are waiting in my room. They are eager to see the question paper that I have designed for my MA students. They see it; they smile; and one of them expresses his feelings with absolute joy: 'It is beautiful. It takes me to the realm of imagination.' How do I respond? A current of emotions overflows my being. I begin to tell him about my engagement, my way of seeing my work. I find myself in a communicative space. Time becomes magical, and it leads me to invoke my wife. True, she left her physical body; yet, the energy she carried envelops my consciousness. And the miracle is that at that very moment I find myself near the majestic Taj Mahal at Agra. My wife looks at a brick with great wonder, and whispers: 'See this small

piece of brick. How beautifully designed it is; so much labour and hard work! Nothing is trivial. Every element has been taken care of. And that is why, the Taj Mahal as a whole is extraordinarily illuminating.' I continue to hear that voice, that language of wisdom. And I tell my student... I have enjoyed—enjoyed immensely—the act of formulating this question paper. I have celebrated it. I have moved around, seen peacocks and butterflies, looked at the sky, read books, and waited and waited. And then suddenly ideas embrace me—the way God appears in silence. I receive the message, and formulate my question paper.

Does my celebration have a meaning in the hard/pragmatic world of academics? Why should a professor spend so much time and energy in designing a question paper? As it is believed, it is just a matter of five minutes. Work on your computer, think for a while about the syllabus you have covered, and type five straightforward questions—define... explain... elaborate.... That's all. A professor is supposed to do great things: writing a scholarly paper, publishing a book, attending a conference, conducting a project, visiting institutions abroad for international collaboration. A professor spending a considerable amount of time and energy in formulating a question paper for the end semester examination, and feeling excited about it—possibly it looks absurd and strange! But then, I deny this

rationale because my wife whispers: 'Recall that brick of the Taj Mahal. Nothing is trivial.' Yes, every small thing—even this question paper, I tell my student, is important. And when you do something that does not have a very concrete and tangible recognition—an award for publications, a position in the academic bureaucracy, a membership in the selection committee, a prime time television appearance, and applause and clapping for a speech in a conference hall—and do it with absolute joy, creativity and seriousness, you find God. Because God is that small thing; God is that ordinary event; God is that naturalness; God is simple. My student, I wish to tell you—everything I do, be it writing a book, or attending a conference or formulating a question paper, is equally important; I do not hierarchize; I see it as a celebration. And that is the way I feel the completeness of my academic life.

Time passes. The examination is over. As I start collecting their papers, a student approaches me. 'Sir, may I say something?' 'Why not?' I ask her to continue. 'Sir, I do not know whether I am brilliant, whether my answers are sufficiently academic and intellectually sound. But Sir, I have allowed my heart to take hold of my pen. For the first time in my life, I am writing an examination in which my heart has played such an important role'. And here is yet another student articulating her

experience with great enthusiasm: 'Sir, thank you very much. You asked a question—what does it to mean to share Rassundari Devi's *Amar Jiban* with one's grandfather? Sir, believe me, I really wanted to share that extraordinary life story—a woman's struggles and aspirations in a patriarchal society—with my grandfather, and feel what it would have meant to him had my own grandmother been a Rassundari Devi.'

I look at them. They surprise me. Even an examination, far from being oppressive, can be a celebration. My mind is filled with joy. I get my reward. I invoke my wife. And this time I whisper in her ears: 'You are right. Nothing is insignificant. Even formulating a question paper is as creative as discovering the law of gravitation!' I come back to my residence, make a cup of tea, open the answer scripts. How wonderful it is to read the experiential writings of these young/vibrant minds:

> If I had narrated Rassundari Devi to my grandfather the first reaction of his would be of discomfort because my grandfather as I know him is a man of authority and dominance. A man who would never tolerate anything or anyone that would challenge his authority so to speak...My reading of *Amar Jiban*would also make him realize the fact that his wife that is my grandmother, might also have undergone the same agony, disappointment and despair as Rassundari Devi. And I think there I would feel successful for at least making my grandfather realize that my grandmother too in some way

> or the other had certain expectations from her husband which my grandfather failed to meet because he was busy meeting the expectations of the society which is essentially patriarchal in nature. Maybe towards the end of the narration when the text would be over and only my grandfather and I would be there, there would be an ambience of silence because we might both be lost in the process of critically reflecting on the text. I would be thinking about my grandmother whose absence would then become the real presence and for my grandfather the same silence would be working as a haunting experience but he would be chased by a guilty conscience for failing to acknowledge what his wife did to her on a regular basis.

Yes, I tell myself, I have succeeded in arousing their imagination. And I feel like whispering in their ears: 'Dear students, you are like those beautiful bricks I need to construct my own Taj Mahal—the Utopia that a teacher loves to visualize.'

2

You should never try to compel someone (because you happen to be a teacher, a supervisor) to read your book; you should not even persuade. If it happens...let it happen naturally, spontaneously, easily—the way a bird comes to a tree.

Visit our Centre. You find a huge board displaying the publications of the faculty: the cover pages of the books written by our professors, reviewed by the well-known experts in the field, and brought out by the publication houses that charm the academic circle. As a matter of fact, it all began with a need to showcase the achievements of our Centre before the UGC committee: how its teachers as dynamic researchers are perpetually contributing to the domain of knowledge, and taking the Centre as well as the university to a great height. The committee came, saw it, and, needless to add, sanctioned the grants.... Yet, the board remains. In fact, with the passage of time new additions make the display more and more attractive. But I ask myself: After the departure of the UGC committee, who are the ones seeing this grand display of our academic creations? Are they our students? It is possible that every morning as they come to the Centre they look at this display, and feel how great their teachers are; they are indeed privileged to be taught by them! Or, is it altogether impossible that we ourselves see our own creations, feel happy, and gratify the irresistible instinct of egotistic pride?

Yes, my books too have been displaced. Something is happening deep inside my consciousness. I am not feeling particularly easy and comfortable. I have a sense of embarrassment. Quite often, as I enter the Centre, my eyes invariably take me near the board, and I begin to feel immensely uneasy. I recall my father who had nothing to do with the high culture of academics. With his characteristic simplicity he used to tell me: 'Never advertise your own achievements. Never display your knowledge as a product. Never talk about yourself.' Have I forgotten my father? Am I seeing him as old-fashioned— a naïve semi-urban gentle man with no idea of how the academic world functions? My discomfort, my uneasiness, my guilt: I feel condemned.

Time passes. The board of display does not seem to have any space left. Possibly in the coming days the Centre has to think of arranging yet another board for showcasing the publications of its professors. After all, our colleagues are dynamic; they write ceaselessly; and big publishers wait for their manuscripts.

But then, one day I acquire the courage. I come to the Centre; I ask a student of mine who, as I feel, understands my dilemma, to accomplish the final act in silence: removing the cover pages of my books from that grand display. Nobody sees it; nor do I inform anybody. I feel relieved. I feel: 'From the clouds my father must have seen this act, blessed me, and my student.' Am I preaching? Am I sounding like an orthodox/ puritan idealist? I do not know. But then, dear students, I wish to tell you something: something very deep that has become part of my looking at my work. True, books are needed; books are desirable; good ideas, good thoughts, good research findings—we must communicate, write books and publish. I too write books; I read books; I love their smell, their touch. But once you write your book, don't advertise it, don't speak too much about it; don't display, commodify, showcase. Your books are in bookshops; your books are in libraries; your books have reached the relevant journals for reviews. You need not bother. Let your books be read, liked, disliked, loved, hated by your readers. Let your publishers do what they feel important to take your books to your potential readers. You create; and then, you forget. Don't hold on. Don't possess. Don't get excessively attached to it. Learn to forget, and laugh at yourself.

Is it the reason that I am becoming increasingly sceptical about book release

functions? Is it the reason that I do not include my own books in the reading list for the courses I teach? Is it the reason that in a seminar/conference while delivering a lecture I do not refer to my own book? Or, is it the reason that I share the experiences of the books I write only with my loved ones: those who understand me and make me grow? Possibly my way of writing or looking at a book does not always fall in line with the way the academic establishment sees it. When I write a book, it becomes my child, my beloved. The entire experience is deeply sacred. Yes, it has its reason, its empiricism, its theories, its discourses, its hard facts, its bibliography, its notes, its indexing, its appendix; yet, for me, the experience remains intimate and aesthetically fulfilling; it refuses to be categorized as just technical and professional. The experience is essentially that of a mother conceiving her child—deeply maternal, feminine and sacred. And if the sacred becomes a product, if it becomes a tool for ego boosting, if it becomes a medium through which I engage in 'networking' and enhance my social capital, it gets profaned; and that is indeed a great loss.

It is of course true that when one reads your book, and communicates that experience with you, you feel good. This feeling is very pure; it is a bond; it is a sense of humility; it is filled with sacred tears. But then, it happens....It cannot be enforced. You should never try to

compel someone (because you happen to be a teacher, a supervisor) to read your book; you should not even persuade. If it happens...let it happen naturally, spontaneously, easily—the way a bird comes to a tree, and converses with it. This means waiting...waiting in silence... waiting with grace...waiting without even being aware that one is waiting. And then, suddenly one fine morning someone gives you a call: 'I have just read your book. It makes me think and feel. I wish to meet you.' That is the moment when that bond takes place, when a writer and a reader communicate, embrace each other. That is a pure moment. That is eternity. Is the culture of waiting disappearing in the world of high academics? Publish, get instant recognition, or perish—that seems to be the mantra driving us to showcase our achievements. Facebook, book release functions, or, for that matter, the display at our Centre—we do not wish to miss any opportunity. We are restless. If our books are not quoted, we feel unhappy. We grow crazy if our PhD students do not include our books in their impressive bibliographies. It seems everything is a theatric play: you are what you present yourself to be, you are your uniform, your mask, your stage performance! You are your book; the more it is talked about the more real you are!

Dear students, I tell you all this because I pray, I pray for you. I want you to write books—

enchanting books. But I do not want you to reduce your creations into products; even academic products, believe me, are nothing but products. I want you to feel easy with your creations, not to get heavily burdened with the baggage of 'name' and 'fame'. And now may I request you to come with me, my dear. See this garden. How beautiful this tiny blue flower is. It attracts you. Its fragrance enters your being. It becomes your soul. It does not promote itself. It does not speak the language of narcissism. It does not have a price tag. It is not conscious of its beauty. And that is why, it is so beautiful. Let the book you write be like this flower. Remember the day when I wrote a brief comment in your classroom diary: 'You are destined to bloom like a flower'.

3

The wonder and mystery of life is that, despite my grey hair, and the constant enquiry about the date of my retirement, my intimate friends are my students. Their fragrance purifies me; their laughter makes me alive; their brilliant questions arouse and stimulate my thoughts; their pain, their aspirations, their dreams, their moments of fall and despair take me to the core of a relationship.

'You are always surrounded by a group of students. I wonder whether they are your chelas: a bunch of sycophants', a fresh MA student once told me. I value his frankness, his clear statement, his wonder, his doubt, his question. In fact, at times, I myself reflect on this relationship. And I realize that I need not justify or defend it. As a matter of fact, I feel good when I am with them; there is so much beauty, laughter, joy and pain in this relationship. Let me narrate what happened the other day. It was a lazy afternoon, and I received a call: 'Sir, may I come to see you for just five minutes?' 'Why not? Please come', I replied. And then he arrived—always pleasant, filled with laughter and joy. 'Here is a gift for you, Sir. Please open it and see it', he persuaded me. I obeyed. Oh, what a wonderful gift! My student, after a long...long search, finally managed to find a poster of *Deewar*—the famous Amitabh Bachchan film I often talk about it in the class. We began to laugh. We cracked jokes. We merged. That is it. My student does not fear me, nor does he retain a distance. He knows—and how often I myself have shared it—that his 'Sir' grew up in the 1970s with Amitabh Bachchan films; he loved *Deewar*, loved Bachchan's intensity in the film, his anger, his deep pain, his longing for his mother. He knows that his 'Sir' does not have any hesitation in admitting his love for some of these Bollywood films. True, I love Ray and Chaplin, Ghatak and Benegal; but this longing for the aesthetics of good and meaningful cinema has never caused heaviness in my being. I have never allowed it to burden me with some sort of cultural capital in my persona. I have my lighter moments. I laugh; I crack jokes; I recite the dialogues of popular Bachchan films. My student knows that. And that is why, the gift makes me feel the lightness of being. A professor becomes a friend; a student becomes an intimate companion. Amitabh Bachchan to Walt Whitman, Herman Hesse to Antonio Gramsci: how beautifully, gracefully we share everything.

Here is the tale of yet another student. Who says that beauty does not exist in the world? Who says that everything about our everydayness is instrumental and calculative? This student of mine loves flowers; he carries their fragrance. Almost every alternative day

he arrives with flowers; and in the freshness of the morning his flowers enter my soul. As he arranges these flowers with absolute patience and aesthetics, I realize the meaning of an action filled with love and creativity. God sends me to the kitchen; I make a cup of tea for him. We talk, laugh and share feelings, experiences and readings. Who is he? A sycophant? Or, a flower? An object in a 'network' society? Or, a fountain of love and care? A research scholar 'serving' his professor? Or, an upward flame of the illuminating light? It is sad that in a cynical environment we feel tempted to see these relationships as calculative and instrumental—a teacher with his 'resources' using his student, or a student 'pleasing' his teacher to gain some profit: a teaching job, a fellowship abroad, a recommendation letter, a good grade! It is equally sad that there are teachers who feel that it is 'distance' that makes them powerful; this distance is legitimated in the name of 'professionalism'. 'Send me an e-mail. Seek an appointment. And the exact date and timing will be communicated to you'—it is not difficult to find professors speaking this language, and erecting a wall separating them from their students. It is really sad that they feel that if they retain a distance, evoke fear, avoid intimacy, they are powerful, they are productive, they are perfect managers of their valuable time. You know me, my dear. My transparent self is before you. If my students

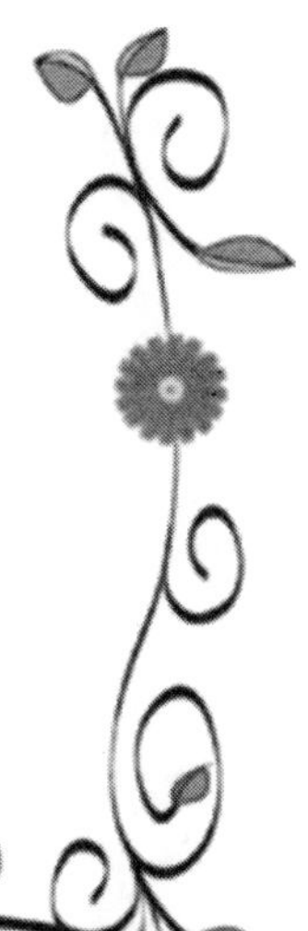

fear me, I would see it as my defeat, my ultimate failure as a teacher. Fear separates; love unites. Distance brings a wall; dialogue brings the souls together. The power of separation causes an illusion of efficiency; Love brings about real work, real efficiency, real dynamism. Love is friendship; love is reverence; love is trust; love is the real power of powerlessness! And one has to feel it. This bond does not trivialize the role of a teacher. Instead, it is the true colour of grace and gratitude. So I give you a call. You will find your answer. My door is open—for you, for everybody. Come. Join the celebration. Have a cup of coffee with me. Share a book, a painting, a story of your being. Who is preventing you, my dear?

'How do you spend time? Who are your friends?' I am often asked this question. My friends are indeed many. I am in touch with my school friends. Suddenly a telephonic conversation—boundless laughter, and recalling the poem a common friend once wrote for his imaginary beloved! My friends are in diverse vocations—in teaching, in administration, in social activism. But the wonder and mystery of life is that, despite my grey hair, and the constant enquiry about the date of my retirement, my intimate friends are my students. Their fragrance purifies me; their laughter makes me alive; their brilliant questions arouse and stimulate my thoughts; their pain, their aspirations, their dreams, their moments of fall and despair take me to the core of a relationship. 'Don't worry, Sir. My doctors are hopeful. I am recovering from cancer'—a student of mine assures me, and I realize what it means to be a teacher. Dear student, possibly you too are going to become a teacher. Celebrate it, celebrate it every moment. Your true power is your love; your real strength is your transparent self; your authentic religiosity is your symmetry with your students. Teaching, believe me, is a deeply spiritual act.

Imagine the magical night at Ranikhet where with some of my students I went for a rhythmic workshop. The post-dinner walk made us see and feel what a seeker strives for—the garland of mountains looking like Sufi mystics, the whisper of those tall pine/oak trees, the curved road, and the vastness of the sky with the radiant moon. We all sat on the road; we remained silent. And then something happened. Since eternity, I felt, we have been walking, walking together. Dear student, do you understand the meaning of this miraculous soundless sound? Feel it, and you will realize what the teacher-taught relationship is all about.

4

The dialogue goes on; you do not stop; you continue your journey; you see with your own eyes; you learn, you unlearn; you fill your minds with all sorts of information; yet, you know how to empty yourself; you exist as a very real, very alive, unique person, despite their books, their fame, their awards. Because you realize that this sunrise is yours, this sunset is your poem, this moon is your magic, this child is your innocence. You are no less important than the books you read.

There is indeed a deep-rooted fear prevailing over the academic culture: the fear of plagiarism. Yes, professors fear that their students are deceiving them; they are not original in their writings, assignments, theses; they are simply copying and engaging in the act of plagiarism. And in the age of mistrust and suspicion it is feared that even some known intellectuals/professors are not altogether free from this vice. So, it is asked, who is blaming whom? Possibly, as a cynic tends to answer, it is a game of mutual deception. I often reflect on this issue. Why is it that in our times this fear/doubt is all-pervasive? Is it because we find ourselves—thanks to the Internet—in the world of abundance—abundance of information, abundance of reading material, abundance of commentaries and reviews, and as a result, we are tempted to borrow and project these ideas as our own? Or, is it because in a recklessly competitive culture we are asked to produce ceaselessly, and write and publish without any limit, and as a consequence, the act of borrowing emerges as an instant solution to the unnatural target that we have posed before ourselves? Yes, all these are possibly true. However, there is something deep about this malice which is not generally talked about. It is in this context that I wish to narrate a story. I remember an incident that happened when I was doing my postgraduation. A professor taught us a course on social stratification. And I studied—and studied reasonably carefully—what the professor wanted us to read: Dumont, Srinivas, Beteille.... Then, one day I asked him: 'Sir, in my term paper is it possible for me to write my own experiential account—the way in the process of growing up in a small town in West Bengal I saw the presence/absence of caste?' 'No, you can't. You are not M.N. Srinivas', my professor reminded me of the 'absurdity' of my wish. I was young and vulnerable. I could not say anything to my professor. Instead, I wrote a 'technically perfect' term paper: nothing original, but full of appropriate quotes and references. And I got a satisfactory grade. However, my professor's remarks continued to haunt me. Today let me share with you—my students—what I wanted to tell my professor. 'Yes, I am not M.N. Srinivas. Why should I be M.N. Srinivas? Or, for that matter, why should I at all try to be M.N.

Srinivas? I am what I am with all my follies and mistakes. Yet, I wish to be an eager learner whose eyes are open, whose mind is alert, who seeks to observe, analyse and interpret the world—not just through the ideas given by celebrity social scientists (even though he adores their scholarship and learns from them), but also through his own experience. I am not dead. Yes, I have tried to read all that you wanted me to read. But then, this reading should not bind me. I ought to have my freedom to learn and unlearn. Why should I be deprived of my right to make mistakes, and yet rise each time I fall? Is everybody in the world—from Srinivas to Beteille—important except my own mind, my own eyes, my own reasoning, my own intuition, my own sensibilities?'

See the deep-rooted malice. As professors we are asking our students to produce 'technically perfect' products. And what is the ideal type of a technically perfect term paper or a dissertation? References... references... references. How frightening it has become! You are compelled to quote. You are not supposed to write anything that cannot be 'substantiated' through the writings of others. See its pathology. 'The sunset is beautiful'—it is not possible to write even this experiential truth without quoting somebody. To quote, it seems, has become your compulsion. You are required to use appropriate vocabulary, give a glossary, and follow a standardized style: say, the style

of a reputed refereed journal. But one thing is certain. You need not bother much about your own thoughts, feelings and experiences. As every student of social science would admit, to write about discipline and power is to refer to Michel Foucault; to write about education is to refer to Bernstein and Bourdieu; to write about nationalism is to refer to Partha Chatterjee and Sudipta Kaviraj; and to write about the Dalit issue is to refer to Gail Omvedt and Kancha Illiah. There is no escape. You are almost compelled to do so. It does not matter whether these references emerge out of your genuine conviction and understanding. Your soul is dead. And you just follow an academic ritual, and your professor as a priest of the discipline is evaluating you on the basis of the perfection of this ritual. What, therefore, emerges is a ritually perfect term paper or a dissertation, but devoid of the fragrance of originality, daring spirit, creativity and those 'mistakes' that make it more real and authentic.

What is this academic product, my dear? Is it original? Or, is it an act of plagiarism, even when not seen as such? The difference, we must be honest enough to accept, is that those who are naïve copy and borrow without acknowledging; and the intelligent ones do the same, but they are perfectly trained in the science of referencing. And what about your professors? You can take a simple test. Ask them to write ten pages—say, on caste, gender,

religion or power—without any reference, without footnotes, without quotes. Ask them to imagine for these ten minutes that no Foucaults, no Marxs, no Durkheims, no Hegels had ever existed in the world. Ask them to imagine that they are discovering everything once again with absolute innocence. Believe me, many of us would not pass this test. The fact is that our words, because of a very inauthentic academic practice, have become ornamental; our ideas are borrowed, and our writings are pretentious. We have lost the courage to remain fresh. One sort of plagiarism is punished; but then, most of our academic practices are nothing but 'legitimate' articulations of plagiarism.

I do not wish to be misunderstood. It is by no means my contention to suggest: 'Don't read.' I am suggesting something deeper. Read, and read intensely and meaningfully. Have a conversation with great writers and researchers. Let your reading be an act of dialogue. As a fellow traveller you are talking to those who too have travelled. You are conversing with Marx while exploring the world produced by capitalism. You are talking to Gandhi and Fanon while you are making sense of the spirit of decolonization. You are sharing great moments with Herbert Marcuse and Walter Benjamin while you are looking at cotemporary mass culture. This dialogue enriches you, it does not restrict you, confine you, burden you, make you a prisoner. The dialogue goes on; you do

not stop; you continue your journey; you see with your own eyes; you learn, you unlearn; you fill your minds with all sorts of information; yet, you know how to empty yourself; you exist as a very real, very alive, unique person, despite their books, their fame, their awards. Because you realize that this sunrise is yours, this sunset is your poem, this moon is your magic, this child is your innocence. You are no less important than the books you read.

There is yet another question that confronts me. As a professor, if I always fear that my students can copy, or borrow words, ideas and even sentences from others, is it altogether impossible for me to give them a different kind of assignment that cannot be copied, that cannot be written even if you give them the entire library—an assignment that demands their own imagination, an assignment that requires authenticity, not cleverness? In fact, this constant fear that our students are expert in plagiarism also reflects our own failure, our poverty of imagination, our inability to intervene meaningfully in the existing pedagogic process. Schools give projects that parents or hired experts do; university professors give assignments (say, an essay on the types of suicide Durkheim talked about; or, a note on Marx's notion of class conflict; or, a review of Foucault's *Madness and Civilization*) that the Internet can do. How tragic it is. Believe it, as teachers we have failed. Yet, I dream. None can deprive me of the joy of dreaming and experimenting. That is my own intimate space, and I value it as a teacher. I am teaching a course entitled *Methods of Social Sciences*. Yes, my students have read a great deal about 'observation'—about Malinowski and Margaret Mead, about their modes of observation, the nuances implicit in the process of observation, the meaning of the observer being observed. But then, I do not feel like asking them to write yet another term paper on 'social anthropology and participant observation'. I know they can write a technically perfect term paper with appropriate notes, quotes and references. But a work of this kind is replaceable. I, therefore, choose to give them an assignment like this:

> Location: Bhikaji Cama Place Crossing. Remain silent and observe—at least for ninety minutes—the continual flow of traffic, the hoardings all around, and above all, the street children engaged in diverse activities. And then, write a sociological essay on 'observation'—its complexities, its multiple layers.

It is simply impossible to copy, to borrow, to impress the professor with big names and their latest publications; the Internet is of no use. What matters is the arousal of creative imagination—the spirit of honest work. And yes, my students realize themselves as creative thinkers; they begin to trust themselves, rather than the Internet or the quotes from Ruth Benedict and Clifford Geertz (even when they

have read and understood their texts). My students, I am convinced, you can make a new beginning. If a challenge is given to you, you feel encouraged to unfold your creativity. And hence I appeal to you to read, and read with great joy. Let books, for you, be enabling, not constraining. Write what you yourself have seen, felt, understood, realized and arrived at. References as such are not bad; there is no harm in quoting others. However, you should quote not to impress, but to have a meaningful conversation with a fellow traveller. And always believe that you matter, you exist, you are unique. Your style is your style. There is no standardized style. There is no *EPW*/OUP style! You create your own style. Have the courage to fail, to fall down, to make mistakes. Yet, trust yourself. I know that you can make it. You can prove that it is possible to create a culture of learning refreshingly free from the fear of plagiarism. After all, how can I forget that it is you, dear students, who have made me realize that even a theory class, far from being a bombardment of names and loaded concepts, can become as rhythmic as a piece of Mozart music?

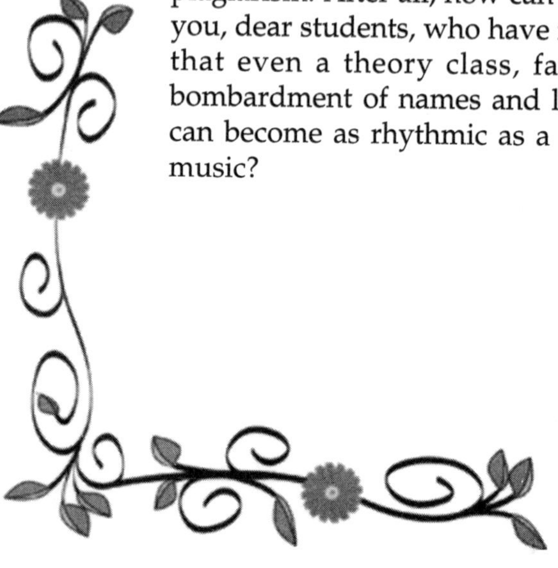

5

Something happens. An invisible force enters my body, my soul. Words, ideas, concepts, analogies and illustrations begin to flow. I have surrendered. I am possessed.

I have taught; I have delivered a lecture—an introductory lecture on the methods of social sciences; I have come back to my chamber; and I see an extraordinarily sacred gift lying on my table—a beautiful picture and a poetic sentence: 'Sir, what a wonderful lecture...poems, Whitman, Satyajit Ray, Weber, Nisbet, science, sociology, Blake...! Isn't methodology becoming engaging and closer to one's reality?' With tears in my eyes, I feel that this morning is truly revealing, and it is through this beautiful gift that God has come to me, and made me realize that I am nothing, my ego is false; I just happen to be a medium through which everybody, every particle spoke, taught, delivered a lecture. It is not this discrete ego—a superficial sense of 'I' with a title/position, with a bio-data, with books and projects—that is teaching; it is essentially the enchanting inspiration nurtured and sustained by God that is teaching. This feeling relaxes me, makes me free; a sense of lightness and joy fills my heart. I begin to see everything.

I see my father taking me to a local school at a small town in West Bengal for admission. I see his eyes: the eyes that see a potential tree in a seed. I see my mother continually encouraging me, and coming to the railway station to see me off as I board the train for Delhi for higher studies. I see her tears of joy. I see my elder brother protecting me, encouraging me to expand, to do meaningful things. I see my friends, their light, their sharpness. I feel their faith, their concern, their positive vibrations. My wife—are you listening? Your physical body might have returned to the earth; but you remain. You remain as a song, you remain as a Himalayan peak, and you remain as the tales that continue to be lived. Are you listening? You possess me as I enter the class. 'Papa, you have to deliver a good lecture', my daughter reminds me as I prepare for the class. She enters my being; I feel God is accompanying me.

Who am I? Who is teaching? Yes, the official record—the record that the university bureaucracy produces every year—would state that Professor Pathak has taught this particular course. But my inner world knows how superficial it is. Because it does not realize that everything happens because of love and connectedness; one carries everybody within oneself. No, I am not teaching; it is through me that all of them are teaching. I wake up quite early in the morning; I see the sun in the eastern horizon; I am inspired. I start for the Centre; I see peacocks and butterflies, they come to me, and enter my being. I go for a walk; a tree whispers; I look above; the radiant moon smiles; ideas begin to strike my imagination; I feel elevated. I read books, listen to music, talk to my daughter, and invoke my wife, my parents. They come and make it possible. My lecture is ready. I come to the class. A foggy morning, shivering cold, 9 am class—yet, all of them are present. They are my flowers; I feel them; their curious eyes, their patience, their penetrating questions and reflections keep me alive. Something happens. An invisible force enters my body, my soul. Words, ideas, concepts, analogies and illustrations begin to flow. I have surrendered. I am possessed. Who is teaching, my dear? This professor is empty, and his emptiness receives you, receives every particle. It is this love that teaches, that delivers a lecture, that communicates, narrates, shares, philosophizes, visualizes.

It happens like this. One day I come back from the class, enter my room; and then, a student of mine arrives, gives me a gift: a literary masterpiece. I begin to value the beauty of studentship—the depths in the relationship between the teacher and the taught. With deep gratitude I open the book, and I see a beautiful passage my student has written in it: 'Sir, you

are my father; you are my Gurudev; you are my philosopher, my guide, my friend.' Tears...only tears; God has knocked on my door. What an intensity in this trust, in this offering, in this prayer! Believe me, I am ordinary, simply ordinary. It is the all-pervading energy—my divine inspiration, my teacher, my bird, my tree, my mountains, my rivers—who make it possible. With deep gratitude and longing I keep the book, hold it softly, and begin to prepare for the next lecture.

6

My students—I am immensely grateful to you. With deep gratitude I recall your gift. A guitar, a melodious voice, a simple, yet profound poem—the song makes me see life. I evolve with it. My sociology evolves; my lecture finds its soul; my romance, my love and my revolution, despite the continual movement of clock time, do not disappear.

How fondly I recall the gift. It was 1992—a group of students gave me a wonderful gift. 'Sir, here is a music cassette for you. We are sure you would love these songs.' With their warmth and assurance I took the gift, and as I started listening to Kabir Suman's extraordinarily beautiful songs, I realized the sensitivity of my students and the worth of a gift. What a magical play of poetic sensibilities and deep feelings emanating from the depths of the inner world! And especially, one of the songs—*Prathomato Tomake Chai*—entered my being, my soul. What a prayer: poetic and political, temporal and transcendental, secular and spiritual! First, I want you. Second, I want you. Third, I want you. Till the end I want you. I want you when I am happy. I want you when I am unhappy. I want you after a long...long walk. I want you when I am tired. I want you in revolutions, in music, in all that is meaningful. Kabir Suman's (who in a way altered the landscape of contemporary Bengali music) enchanting voice, the poetry in his music, its soul, its everydayness, yet its realm of transcendence: everything touched me. I evolved a relationship with the song.

And it seems that there is something eternal about this relationship. I love its romanticism. I love its religiosity. I love its nuanced narratives of everyday life. I love its ability to transcend the duality of politics and prayer. It gives me a call; it inspires; it enhances my longing; it makes my tears deeply sacred. In a way this song has become my biography. Did my students have the third eye to see it? I felt this song at every moment—after reading a good book, after delivering a lecture, after seeing a beautiful film, after smelling the fragrance of early morning in the high altitudes of Uttarakhand, after sharing a cup of tea with my loved ones, after experiencing a flowing river, after pain, after anxiety, after revelation.... It kept my wonder, my romance alive. I could feel. I could love. I could cry. I was indeed enchanted. But then, one day things turned upside down....

Yet, the song remained as my intimate companion. Because at a deeper level nothing that is eternal disappears; forms change, but the essence remains. The singer's 'You' became my song, my flower, my mountain peak, my cherished utopia, my living history, my occultism, my faded manuscript, my books, my lectures, my kitchen, my smell. My students—I am immensely grateful to you. With deep gratitude I recall your gift. A guitar, a melodious voice, a simple, yet profound poem—the song makes me see life; I evolve with it. My sociology evolves; my lecture finds its soul; my romance, my love and my revolution, despite the continual movement of clock time, do not disappear.

2013: I am with yet another group of students. We are concluding the course which I have taught in the monsoon semester with a cultural programme. And see the miracle. As the programme is about to end, they play the same song. Tears in my eyes. What else do I do? The singer is not separated from me. He utters my voice, communicates my melody. Yes, I want you. I want you all the time. I want that feeling, that assurance, that intensity, that religiosity, that touch, that love. And at this very moment I want you—in this room where my students are organizing the cultural programme. In all my creations, in all my aspirations I want you. Do my students understand it? Who knows? It is a miracle. 1992-2013: one miracle leads to another.

My students who gave me the gift in 1992 have grown up; they are well-settled; they are scattered in different parts of the world. And after twenty- two years I am engaging with yet another group of students. Yet, the song remains, love remains. How can something that

is eternal die? With this song I keep moving; my journey continues; I see places, read books, write ideas, meet people, discover the oceans in the eyes of my students, encounter difficulties, pain and struggle. But that 'You'—the mystery of the divine interplay of time and timelessness, form and formlessness, historical and mythical, earthly and heavenly—accompanies me. Yes, I want you. I want you at every moment. How can I exist without you?

January, 2014. I have just returned to my residence after a long evening walk. The cold wave, its mystery and the rhythm of my footsteps: Kabir Suman whispers in my ears. I begin to breathe the song. I want you. I want you. I want you. Where are you—my mother, my wife, my God, my flower, my soul, my Himalayan peaks, my mythology, my epic? I look at the sky. The moon has just begun to arrive. I have found you. I feel that I will continue to find you. My love has not dried up. My romance has not disappeared. Dear students, can a teacher exist without the abundance of love and romance?

7

There is an element of indeterminacy in life. That is the wonder, the surprise. That makes life mysterious. And that is why, there are limits to 'methods'. Learn methods. But at the same time, be aware of their limitations. That makes you humble. That transforms you—from a technically efficient scientific observer with a carefully drafted 'research design' to a humble wanderer.

It was quite an unusual class. It was 9 am—a foggy winter morning. Its implicit mysticism created an ambience that led us to assemble at the Partha Sarathy Rock—a beautiful space inside the university campus surrounded by rocks, an open air theatre, and above all, an expanded horizon. We thought that we would feel the space, smell the fragrance of cold breeze, look at the vast sky—the play of the dark clouds, and discuss all that we were studying in a course relating to the methods of social sciences. Yes, the abundance of nature touched us. Limits were transcended; the culture of learning was acquiring a poetic vision; the mundane nature of everydayness was becoming sacred.

The class began. Rocks, trees, birds, clouds were witnessing. But then, something happened. It started raining.... Should we then run, run faster, go back to the normal classroom: the sanitized 250 sq ft space with its four walls, neon light, television screen and air conditioner? 'No', suggested a student. 'There is a room behind the open air theatre. Sir, let's move there', he added. We followed him. It was a small room—not very clean. Yet, at that moment our inner cleanliness was more than sufficient to take that room which, despite its darkness and cave like structure, emerged as our dialogic space. We began.... It was a discussion class: a discussion on a methodological riddle on which I had already delivered a lecture. It was about 'structure', 'structuralism', and 'structuration'. To put it in simple words, while travelling through the ideas of the luminaries like Emile Durkheim, Louis Althusser, Levi Strauss, Alfred Schultz and Anthony Giddens we were enquiring whether our actions were determined by something called 'social structure'—its institutionalized pattern, its orderly arrangement of 'status' and 'role', its codified principles, laws and sanctions; or whether, irrespective of differences in cultural manifestations, there was an underlying 'structure' in our mind (continually operating in terms of the play of binary opposites like 'raw' and 'cooked', 'hot' and 'cold', 'up' and 'down') 'explaining' all our deeds; or whether, despite the prevalence of 'structure', we too—as creative/reflexive beings— could give meanings to our actions leading to the process of 'structuration': a creative and dialectical interplay of 'structure' and 'agency'.

My students were ready to comment, to converse, to make their observations. They were looking at their notes, referring to Durkheim and Giddens, summarizing their arguments, and adding new insights. Meanwhile, rains...more rains... thunderstorm: the room was getting darker. Yet, there was light in the darkness—the light emanating from all these young/vibrant students. A student began with an interesting observation. 'Sir, see how the 'structure' operates. Tuesday 9 am. As the time-table—the codified rule of the university—suggests, you are required to take the class, and as students we are compelled to attend it. That is the way the 'structure' has defined us. And see the weather. It is severely cold; it is raining. Yet, we can't escape the overwhelming power of the 'structure'. You have to take the class. And we have to attend it.' What a beautiful point. An example emanating from the experiential domain of this very moment—not a high sounding quote from a book mechanically recited. Theory became experiential; philosophy touched the being; learning became an inner awakening.

She inspired. I could see the smiling faces. They began to speak. I allowed myself to listen, listen carefully. And then I spoke: 'Yes, my student. How right you are. There is indeed a 'structure' that has arranged us—teachers and students—in a manner that is institutionalized, codified; it is almost like a 'thing' existing out

there with its time-table, course-instructor, registered students, assignments, credit system, evaluation, grading and official certification. Our freedom, you are right, is not that of a bird flying in the sky. As historically located actors, we are bounded. I agree with you—my student. The rains, the thunderstorm, the shivering cold are not yet powerful enough to alter the 'script' (as a teacher, I teach; as a student, you attend my class) that the 'structure' of the university as a 'social system' has already written for us. Yet, I wish you to see something more. We are redefining the script. Isn't it? True, we are within the 'structure'; yet, from within we are altering, changing and modulating it. The class is not taking place in the allotted lecture hall sanctified by the 'official' time-table. The venue of this class is what the 'structure' has never dared to imagine. And hence we too are emerging as creators, skilled performers; we are not just passive role-performers. Yes, it is a theatre with a director, a script, an allocation of roles; yet, it is an alive theatre that innovates itself every moment, that perpetually negotiates with the script, with the director—a theatre that is a process, a continual process. And what else is 'structuration',my dear?'

Their eyes were filled with wonder and curiosity. Durkheim and Giddens were coming out of thick books, term paper footnotes, and fashionable bibliographies. They were merging with the rains, with the rocks, with the sky. My

students were learning; learning was becoming a celebration. It was 11 am. The rains had already stopped. A song, a poem by Rlike, and then, we all moved towards our 'official' location.

It was quite late in the afternoon. I was discussing with a group of students in my office room. One of them asked: 'Sir, this morning was beautiful. But tell me Sir, how do you explain the sudden rainfall?' The question filled my mind with joy. And I replied: 'I am happy that you have asked this question. You see I feel the sudden rainfall as a messenger through which God has sent his message: Be aware of your planning. There are limits to our planning. We thought that we would take the class under the open sky. We did not predict the rains. But then, the rains turned our plan upside down. We had to seek refuge inside a tiny room. So please realize that there are limits to planning; there is an element of indeterminacy in life. That is the wonder, the surprise. That makes life mysterious. And that is why, there are limits to 'methods'. Learn methods. But at the same time, be aware of their limitations. That makes you humble. That transforms you—from a technically efficient scientific researcher with a carefully drafted 'research design' to a humble wanderer. And believe me, only when you are a humble wanderer you see and experience the deeper reality.'

The discussion was over. As I was coming

back to my residence, a strange thought came to my mind. I felt like shouting: 'Mr. Vice-Chancellor. The choice is yours. You can suspend me for bringing the analogy of rains, thunderstorm, sky, clouds, music, poetry in an academic lecture, and that too in a discussion on 'methods'. Or, you can join me, join my students, celebrate the rains, look at the sky, and feel what every educationist needs to realize: Nature is our best tutor!'

8

You find the nuances of social reality—not necessarily always by following 'methods'; you find it at moments when your research design has failed, your structured questionnaire has become incapable of going deeper, and something unexpected happens—an outburst of laughter, a joke, some intense moments of silence, tears in reddish eyes, an accident, a death, a traumatic memory. Be prepared for these surprises.

Yes, in my class I dare to recite a poem and tell a ghost story, even when I am acutely aware of the fact that my students are young researchers pursuing a course on the methods of social sciences, and many of them will eventually emerge as professional sociologists, forget poetry, abhor the romance of innocence, and with their 'adult like maturity' love to speak a heavily loaded language taking its vocabulary from the likes of Bourdieu, Rorty and Derrida. Yet, I dare. And I feel immensely happy that my academics have not yet been able to diminish what William Blake would have categorized as 'songs of innocence'. I teach methods. I teach all that the high culture of academics wants me to do: how to think 'rationally'; how to see the epistemological roots of 'induction' and 'deduction' in Francis Bacon and Rene Descartes respectively; how to get enriched by Karl Popper's theory of refutability, or Thomas Kuhn's path-breaking ideas on 'normal science', 'paradigm' and 'puzzle solving'; how to construct a hypothesis for validation; how to formulate a questionnaire and an interview schedule; how to conduct a 'focus group interview'; how to engage in the act of sampling, select respondents and informants, and use statistical techniques for measuring, tabulating and quantifying empirical data; how to experience the science of hermeneutics—from Dilthey to Gadamer, and interpret the cultural domain of symbols, meanings and texts; or how to go through ethnography, and learn the lessons of 'field work' from Malinowski and Evans Pritchard, Clifford Geertz and M.N. Srinivas.

Yet, I dare. And hence I ought to reflect on the poetic vision which is seldom found in the language of academics, in its obsession with 'methods'—with its belief that there is a road to truth, and if you learn to read the map of the road, you can surely arrive; the belief that if you know the grammar of English you can invariably write like Blake and Whitman; the belief that truth knocks on your door only when you are prepared with your tools and techniques of research. But the poet said something else. The entire day, as the poet began, we made beautiful arrangements, we made appropriate plans, we prepared ourselves. Yet, He didn't arrive. All our thoughts, designs and structures failed. We

gave up. If He didn't arrive in day light, if He didn't arrive when we were prepared, how could He arrive at this odd hour, in this silence of dark night? Then, suddenly a knock at the door, a sound of footsteps...; we didn't bother; we felt that it was the wind, the thunderstorm.... We didn't realize that He had actually arrived.

What a great poem! I wanted my students to feel it. I wanted them to realize that there are limits to 'methods', there are limits to our research designs, there are limits to the methodological certainty that professors seek to inject in their minds: 'Be scientific. Overcome your biases. Choose the proper site—your 'field'. Decide your 'primary' and 'secondary' sources. Use right techniques. And you are bound to get it.' No, it doesn't happen like this. You find the nuances of social reality—not necessarily always by following 'methods'; you find it at moments when your research design has failed, your structured questionnaire has become incapable of going deeper, and something unexpected happens—an outburst of laughter, a joke, some intense moments of silence, tears in reddish eyes, an accident, a death, a traumatic memory. Be prepared for these surprises. Yes, the poem gave me the language to articulate this point. Sorry, my colleagues, I love to recite poems in the methodology class.

And then one day as my lecture gained its momentum, I began to tell them a ghost story.

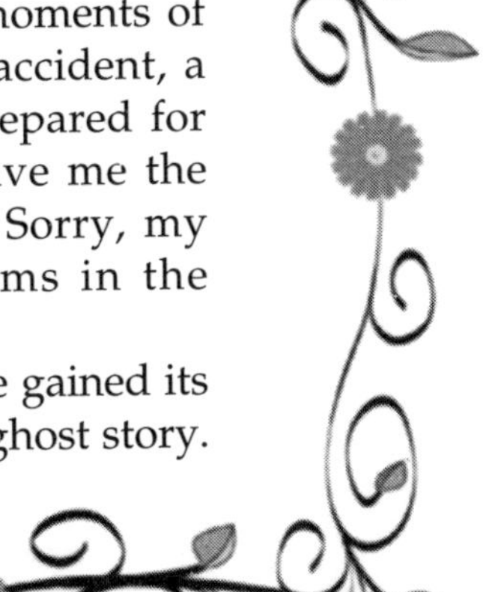

Was it superstitious? Was I insulting the rationality of intelligent JNU researchers? I don't know. But let me narrate how it happened. I was delivering a lecture on diverse modes of engagement between the knower and the known in sociological research. While referring to the writings of Emile Durkheim, Max Weber and Alvin W. Gouldner, I was trying to make them see the three possible modes of engagement often discussed and talked about. First, it is said that a sociologist as a 'value-neutral' professional ought to retain a distance from his/her respondents; this 'distance', it is argued, helps to objectify the social reality, see it as hard data, and retain the rigour of 'scientific explanation'. Second, there is yet another argument. Yes, distance is needed; it helps one to see facts as facts; yet, it should not be forgotten that social facts are not just 'things'; there are deep meanings and experiences implicit in these facts; and it is, therefore, important to cultivate the skill of 'empathy' so that the sociologist can imagine himself/herself in the position of the actor, and understand the meaning intended by him or her. And third, it is argued that the sociologist's 'self' too should play a creative role in research, in this engagement with the field; 'reflexivity' breaks 'methodological dualism', and enables the researcher to realize that to know the world is to know oneself. Knowledge is not just information; it is also an awakening.

My lecture was gaining its momentum, and I was about to conclude. And then, I felt that I must end with a ghost story. I began to narrate.... I was engaging with a group of children and their parents dislocated from Jharkhand, Chhattisgarh and Bihar, earning their livelihood as construction workers, and living in poorly constructed/unhygienic huts inside the campus. Yes, 'distance' and my 'professional gaze' were more than sufficient to gather some hard facts and data, and place them in neatly devised sociological categories: urbanity, migration, displacement, daily wages, and malnourished children somehow managing to attend poor quality government schools. But then, something happened. Looking at these children I felt that I too was a child, and as a child I always waited for someone—maybe my elder sister, my father, my mother—to tell me a ghost story; I wanted to experience the thrill of fear and joy. Are these children different simply because they are the children of construction workers? Are they just my empirical 'data'? My question took me to the domain of reflexivity, and then everything changed. It was a foggy winter night and we were shivering. An ideal moment for a ghost story, and I rediscovered myself as a story teller. What a joy! All these children who, till now, were mere data, began to come closer; they touched me, and in that touch I experienced their thrill mixed with fear and joy, belief and

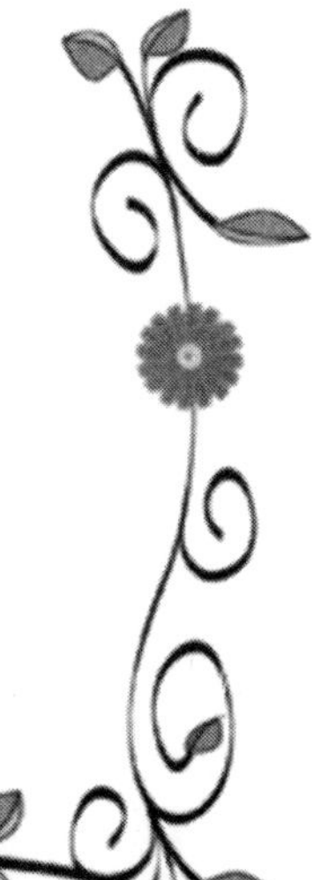

unbelief. 'Pathakji, you have to tell another story. Please...please come again', I received my gift. Distance was broken. With empathy and reflexivity I began to enter their world; I began to understand; I began to feel yet another engagement between the knower and the known.

I could not resist the temptation. I narrated the entire incident and repeated the same ghost story in my class. Boundless joy and laughter in the class. Yes, it was laughter, pure laughter. Sorry, sorry all the authors of the 'prescribed' textbooks of research methodology—you didn't teach me how to tell a ghost story, or recite a poem. Yet, it happened, and acted as a miracle. So, my students—come, come near me; hold my hand; let us begin yet another poem, another ghost story...

9

I wake up. 9 am class. I acquire the courage to come to our garden, smell the fragrance of a flower, pluck it, take it with me, walk towards the university, enter the lecture hall, see my students, feel the light, and give them the flower—my gift, my Universe.

I know that there are many occasions when I have failed, failed as a teacher, as a friend, as an elderly comrade. And these moments of failure make me pass through a dark tunnel. I experience many emotions: anger, fear, pessimism, a sense of defeat and withdrawal. I cease to inspire. No, I need not pretend; I need not deny; I acknowledge this fall, this failure. And possibly this failure is a reminder: 'Never think that you have achieved. You have your limitations, your weaknesses. True, you are a teacher; but even for a second don't think that you have ceased to become a student.' I receive the message, and I begin to pray: 'Let the sun rise once again and illumine my being after this terrible darkness.'

Binsar—a Himalayan hamlet in Uttarakhand—is a narrative of extraordinary illumination. With a group of students I move around Binsar. High altitude, dense forest,

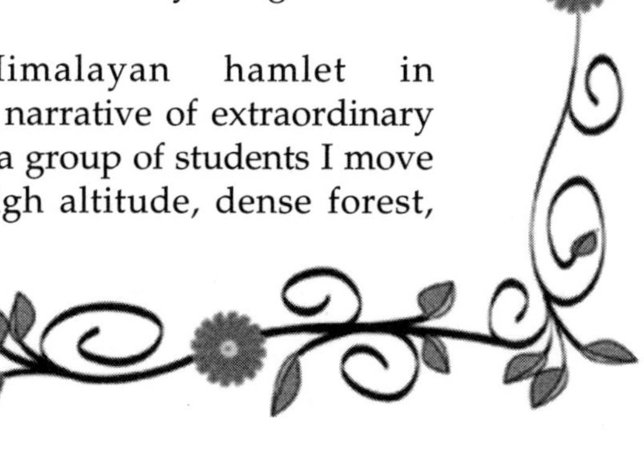

snow peaks, whisper of trees, stars in the revealing sky, infinite void, and deep...deep silence—nature heals, nature teaches, nature evokes poetry. And we are at Binsar to feel the mountains, to experience the trees, to merge with this soundless sound, and to reflect on poetry: not just as the rhythm of written words, but the poetry of the inner world—our intense moments of love, longing, pain, solitude and prayer. We are at Binsar to realize our innate potential—to give and hence to receive, to communicate, to nurture one another. Not as insulated/atomized/egocentric individuals burdened with all sorts of complexity and negativity, but as humble wanderers, as fellow travellers holding one another's hands, understanding, communicating, receiving, giving, loving and radiating the waves of sublime poetry—our journey begins with this aspiration.

Yes, we are finding, finding what a seeker strives for—the sun kissing, and kissing with such tenderness, the snowy peaks, a rhythmic walk through the woods, the melancholy of the sunset, the play of colours in the sky, its music; and we find our poems: some intimate/pure moments in our biographies; we eat together—reading and sharing our diaries, and feeling the ecstasy of togetherness. Yet, amidst all these positive vibrations, something has begun to happen. From the peak we fall down; from our inner beauty we come back to what society regards as our 'normal' selves—negative talk, gossip, internal rivalry, miscommunication, indifference, symbolic violence. A flower has just begun to bloom; but it is sad that we are destroying it. We have just begun to realize that God is this abundance, this extraordinary beauty, this silence, this depth; but it is unfortunate that we cannot bear it any more; we do not believe our own eyes, we condemn ourselves, we become limited, fragmented, divisive, negative.

It is happening. I feel it. I have already experienced many ventures of this kind—largely with a great degree of fulfilment and satisfaction. This possibly made me proud. But now God is teaching me the lesson: 'Your pride is false. Your vanity is the reason for your fall. You have overestimated yourself.' Yes, I fall down. I lose my temper. I tell my students: 'Forgive me. This is my last venture. I am withdrawing. I can't bear it any more.' Something happens. My fall shocks them, surprises them. Possibly they thought that somehow their 'Sir' would be able to retain his calm, manage things and restore order. But something else is happening. Like a dejected/defeated being I am sinking, negativity is enveloping me, I am thinking that it is not possible to work in a group because we are essentially selfish and wicked. I crumble. I am almost dead. At this juncture, things begin to take a different turn. They all come to my room.

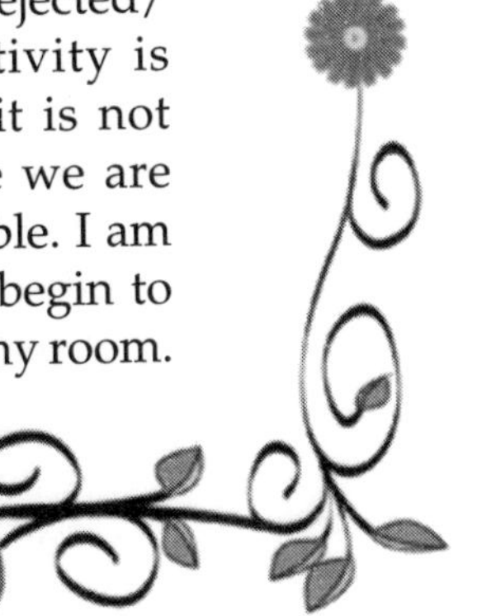

They cry. They apologize. And a reversal of roles takes place. They become my tutors, my guardians. My eyes are closed. Their words reach my ears: 'Sir, you have brought us together. You are the connecting link. You are our source of inspiration. It is you who have told us that we can fall down, but our divinity lies in our ability to rise once again.'

I try. I fail. I start walking through the woods. And then I happen to see two of my students. A leaf has just fallen from a huge tree. They take the leaf, and give it to me. Their gift touches my being. They become my mothers. I become their child. I cannot control myself. I begin to cry—tears of joy, tears of longing. There is lightness in my being; I now see the snowy peaks once again. We come back. Discussion, reflection, sharing—it continues. For some, the mind is still heavy; the wound does not heal easily. For some, the healing process has begun. And what about my own state of consciousness? I know it is not easy. I become alert. However, there are three reminders that convey a deep message to me. First, as human forms we are deeply ambiguous: a constant battle is taking place between our limitedness and our innate potential for experiencing the infinite, between our egotistic self-centredness and our urge to love and melt, between despair and the glimpse of light. The battle does not end. But then, there is no reason to give up. It is this epic battle, it is this struggle for rising, for unfolding our goodness, our innate potential that gives a meaning to our existence. Second, the moment you emerge from your shell, begin your journey, it evokes reactions. You are liked; you are disliked. You are praised; you are condemned. We tend to get paralyzed by someone's negative remarks, harsh words. This negativity provokes us, and we too become negative. But then, this is a trap. We allow ourselves to be caught in this vicious circle. At this juncture, I begin to feel that we must continue to walk, remain dialogic, and do what our conscience permits. We should not be unduly affected by praises or condemnations. Third, there seems to be no other way than love. We all wish to be loved, healed and nurtured. So if I want love, why should I not give it to others? Yes, there is always a fear—if you care, if you love, if you spread out, if you melt, if you do not show your 'power' you are likely to be exploited. But who would exploit whom? When I hate someone, when I generate negativity around me, I exploit myself because I do not allow myself to evolve, to elevate; instead, I sink, I degenerate. Moreover, if I love you, what will you deprive me of? My wealth, my possession, my power, my ego? In fact, when love overflows, wealth, power, possession, ego—everything becomes secondary, meaningless. Take everything from a lover; yet, a lover gives because to love is to experience the infinite.

All these flashes of truth strike me. I seek to rise. And then comes yet another sunrise, another morning. I find an envelope. I open it. What a wonderful gift! A student of mine has written a letter, articulated her dilemmas, struggles, confusions, yet her constant urge to see the golden light. And she concludes the letter with a beautiful poem:

Yes, my child, go out into the world; walk slow
And silent, comprehending all, and by and by
Your soul, the Universe, will know
Itself: the Eternal I.

I wake up. 9 am class. I acquire the courage to come to our garden, smell the fragrance of a flower, pluck it, take it with me, walk towards the university, enter the lecture hall, see my students, feel the light, and give them the flower—my gift, my Universe.

10

True, in this ongoing play of interpretation there is no absolute truth, no objective/foundational knowledge; but then, what emerges is no less beautiful; it is a journey: an artist with colours shaping, changing, adding, deleting, altering the landscape she is painting. It is not perfect mathematics; but it is nearer to life because life too evolves, grows, waits for surprises.

As I teach a course entitled *Methods of Social Sciences*, I am obliged to deliver a series of lectures on what is known as the *hermeneutic* method—a process of understanding and interpreting meanings, actions, symbols and texts. In a way, it is what my profession demands; I ought to tell my students how and why this mode of interpretation and understanding gained importance—how it makes us aware of the fundamental distinction between natural sciences and cultural sciences, why law-like generalizations and explanations that characterize natural sciences are not necessarily always applicable to the study of cultural life because humans are subjective/reflexive, they attach meanings to their world, they create symbols, languages and mythologies that require a deeper understanding, not a ruthlessly homogenized process of scientific reductionism. Yes, I prepare myself; I orient myself; I familiarize myself with the genealogy of the entire tradition; I tell them about Dilthey, Heidegger and Gadamer; I make them see how the art of understanding is immensely interesting, yet a complex process, how it begins to shake our belief in certainty, in objective/foundational knowledge, how it creates a world filled with the plurality of interpretations generating a possibility of relativism and indeterminacy. The debate goes on; students read, argue, write their assignments.

Yet, something happens. I keep asking myself: Is it only an academic question? Is it only about the methods of social sciences? The question disturbs me. And then slowly I begin to realize that this urge to understand, or this need to understand, or this aesthetic play of understanding is essentially about life—not just the preoccupation of professional social scientists. For some time I allow myself to remove these texts from my sight; I seek to unlearn; I wish to regain that simplicity, that curiosity, that intuitive flash through which I understand why a flower is looking at me and smiling, I understand the stories hidden inside the eyes of my daughter, I understand the act of my student when she comes with a book, and says 'Sir, I read parts of this book and I loved it; I felt like sharing this book with you.' I understand; indeed, I understand. Who bothers about theory? I understand; that's all. Is my understanding a 'right' understanding? At this moment, that is not my question. I feel I understand, and this understanding leads me to an act of deep communion. The flower talks to me; my daughter's eyes make me pray for her spiritual elevation; my student's act makes my hand touch her head with deep love and blessing. Life becomes oceanic.

My urge to understand does not end. How can it end? To live is to expand, to meet people, to come across historical characters, to experience literary narratives, artistic creations and symbols. Do I succeed? Do I always understand? I do not know. But the play goes on; it has its own beauty, mystery and thrill. I move. I come across a historical character like Mohandas Karamchand Gandhi. Through my historical imagination I see him in his prayer meetings; I hear his voice, his cross-religious dialogue. Do I understand? Or do I see it as just a fact, a hard archival fact, a soulless information? History, for me, is not a chronicle of facts and events; instead, history whispers, history sings, history touches, history acquires a soul. I seek to understand. I am not Gandhi; my upbringing is different from that of Gandhi. I live in a different time; I feel tempted to speak a language that is 'rational' and 'secular'. Does it then mean that I can never understand Gandhi? Does it then mean that, instead of understanding, I can only impose my categories on him? No, I don't do that. I become humble

and alert. I familiarize myself with Gandhi's biography; I try to feel the turbulent history Gandhi was passing through; and then with the power of my imagination I enter his prayer meeting. I listen. I receive. I do not impose. And then possibly an act of communion begins to take place. I understand why, for him, man's inner world is important; why, for him, the purification of the soul leads to compassion; why, for him, religiosity is not a sectarian dogma, but an ethical quest that characterizes all great religious leaders, be it Krishna or Christ, the Prophet or Nanak. I understand why at that painful time of religious/communal divide, Gandhi's prayer meeting was like the much desired raindrop in a deserted land; I feel the healing touch.

Life moves... From history I come back to my everydayness. I meet people—friends, relatives, strangers. They seek to understand me. I try to understand them—not necessarily always consciously—their gestures, their experiences, their symbols, their narratives. I am in a super-speciality hospital. My student is struggling in the Intensive Care Unit; she is about to die. I see her husband. I see her daughter, their only child. She is not talking; there is immense silence, pain, depth in her being, in her eyes. Do I understand her? My lived experiences take me back to 2009. My wife was in yet another hospital—her last moments, her departure, and our only daughter's pain, silence and hidden tears. Everything becomes one. I understand—believe me, I understand—what my student's daughter is passing through.

But then, do I understand those things about which I have no lived experience? I am not a woman; I am not a Muslim. As an upper caste/ Hindu man I have never experienced what my student passes through every day. Yes, society looks at her 'Muslim' identity; she is subject to some sort of surveillance. She covers her head; and the security person at the metro station would invariably give her a suspicious look, search her belongings, and scrutinize her thoroughly, whereas others who look 'normal' would not pass through the similar experience. She is not 'normal'; she is a stereotype; a potential threat to the nation! She narrates her experiences, the story of her humiliation. Can I understand it? Even though I do not have a lived experience of it, I move, I expand; my empathy, my intuition make me somewhat nearer to her experience. I see it as a human possibility. I see it as the ultimate human strength that enables us to see beyond our limited horizons, and feel what happens elsewhere. In fact, it was she who once told me: 'Sir, see the amazing power of Rabindranath Tagore. It seems he has experienced all sorts of emotions; it appears he has lived the lives of every character he has created.' Yes, she is right. An artist carries that strength so deeply. Tagore understands the spiritual churning of Gora;

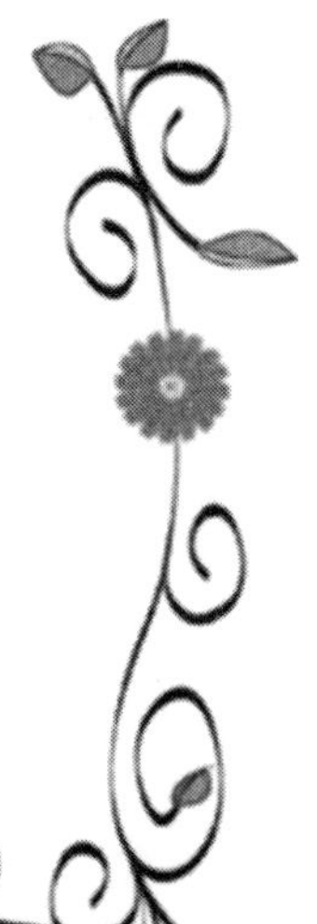

Premchand understands the agony of Dukhi, and Marx understands the pain of an alienated worker. Each of us is a potential artist. To understand, to feel, to relate, to touch, to expand is to cultivate the quality of an artist implicit in each of us. Understanding is indeed a process of artistic play.

Does understanding necessarily mean acceptance of one's act? Not really. I understand you—your historicity, your context, your psychic experience, your compulsion, your aspirations; but it does not necessarily mean that I accept what you do. Let me begin with an example. My destiny makes me engage with a builder who is expected to deliver me a small cottage in a beautiful Himalayan hamlet. I pay him, give him the instalments in advance with the hope that he will deliver the cottage in due time. However, things take a different turn. He breaks promises after promises; he invents excuses; he lies; and eventually, he refuses to accept my phone call; he does not reply to my mail. Yes, I grow angry; I feel cheated; I begin to feel that he is taking advantage of my 'softness'; he has taken me for granted; he is exploiting me. I feel like becoming hard, taking legal action. Yet, there are moments when, despite my anger, my definition of the builder as a liar, I ask myself: Why is it that he is behaving like this? I seek to understand him. And I keep imagining: possibly he does not take my call because he feels ashamed, because he

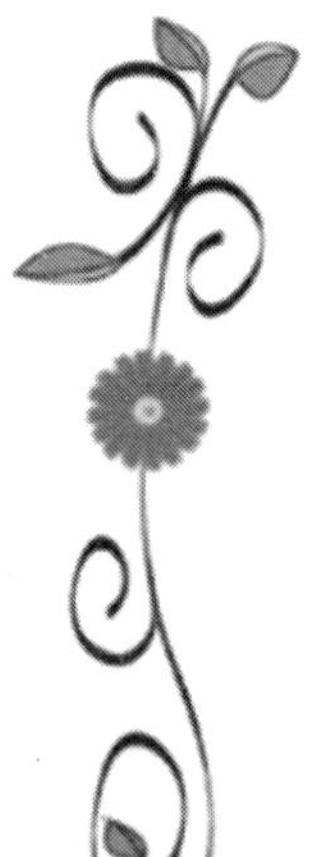

does not have the courage to face me; or possibly he has suffered a severe financial loss which happens to businessmen quite frequently because of their never-ending greed, or he has invested the money collected from people like us somewhere else, and hence he is not in a position to complete the construction work and deliver the cottage. I begin to see him through his eyes. That does not mean that I give my consent to his act. But then, this very act of understanding, under these heavily hostile/ unpleasant circumstances, begins to teach me a couple of lessons. I do not know what happens to the builder; but something happens to me. I realize that I ought to have patience; I ought to have some control over my anger, and I ought to try once more to convey a message to him: 'Mr. Builder, you can discuss your difficulties freely. I am willing to give you some time and space before I decide to take legal action. But please don't hide, don't lie, don't give yet another excuse, don't run away. Trust your higher self. You can fulfil the promise, no matter how difficult your circumstances are.' And I also realize—through my own experience of being cheated—how important it is to keep the trust alive in life. My understanding of the builder does not lead me to accept his act; but this very urge to understand enriches me as a human being.

Life poses these challenges time and again. For example, I do not approve of terrorism; but

I seek to understand the situation of a terrorist. What is it that compels a young man (who too like many other young people must have fascination for love, beauty, sexuality, art and sports) to take up guns and bombs and play with death? I do not approve of the act of a rapist. But I seek to understand: What is it that makes him incapable of experiencing love as a gift of reciprocity, as a poetic rhythm, as tenderness, as a divine touch, as the union of bodies and souls producing enchanting *ragas*? Why is it that for him a woman is only flesh, an object of gross pleasure? Why is it that someone's pain and humiliation fulfils his masculinist ego? As I begin to understand—even though I condemn his act, something happens. I realize that the aggression of a rapist or the nihilism of a terrorist is not something that exists out there; it might lie within me, and my psychic/spiritual evolution lies in my ability to overcome this negativity, and realize my oceanic love. In other words, understanding others is always self-understanding.

It is this act of understanding that makes me sensitive to the possibility of plurality of interpretations. How often it happens. I watch a film, read a poem, listen to a song; I find my own meaning; my interpretation is something that is very intimate to me. But then, as I share my interpretation with my friends and colleagues, I see that their interpretations do not necessarily always converge with mine. While

I do not undervalue my own interpretation, I become aware that it is not proper to absolutize my position. I can engage; I can debate; I can learn; I can unlearn. In other words, my interpretation is not something static; it evolves and grows; it is a continual process. True, in this ongoing play of interpretation there is no absolute truth, no objective/foundational knowledge; but then, what emerges is no less beautiful; it is a journey: an artist with colours shaping, changing, adding, deleting, altering the landscape she is painting. It is not perfect mathematics; but it is nearer to life because life too evolves, grows, waits for surprises. Another thing happens. I interpret a poem, a painting, a religious text; but my interpretation need not resemble what the poet or the painter or the author intended. Does it then mean that my interpretation has no validity? It is not like that. The text transcends its author; it is now subject to multiple readings and interpretations. And who knows that at times the author herself might get enlightened by the reader's interpretation? Not solely that. The fact that I can have my engagement with, say, a William Blake, or a Rabindranath Tagore, or the *Bhagavad Gita* frees me from the tyranny of 'experts'. My Tagore is my Tagore; even though I am always willing to grow, I do not wish to be dictated by a literary critic, a Tagore expert, or a professor of literature. I do not bother about the 'correct' interpretation. I find my Tagore at

the moment of my pain, my deep longing, my love, my ecstasy, my solitude, my darkness. I value it. I do not know whether I am legitimating relativism. But I wish to believe that I too exist.

There is always a possibility of what we regard as 'misunderstanding'. Everyone seeks to be understood and listened to. However, we often realize that we are not understood; instead, we are judged, evaluated and condemned. I am seeing the mountain peaks; I wish to be alone; I wish to be in a deep communion with these peaks. But my friend grows angry. He complains: 'You are avoiding me. You are showing an attitude.' I feel bad. Why is it that my friend is not understanding me? I am not self-centred; I am not avoiding him; instead, being alone for some time is my deep existential need, my prayer; it arouses all that is beautiful in me that, I believe, would also illumine my friend. But my friend, I am afraid, does not understand me. I am unhappy, sad. For me, it is misunderstanding. We live with this rapture, this gap, this broken communication. Do we understand ourselves? How often we realize that we are ignorant of our own actions. The fact is that this actor/performer/doer in me is not always a concretely defined, stable, coherent agent. There are many layers inside us—partly known , partly unknown. We surprise ourselves: 'Oh, it is me. Even I could do that.' That surprise or that

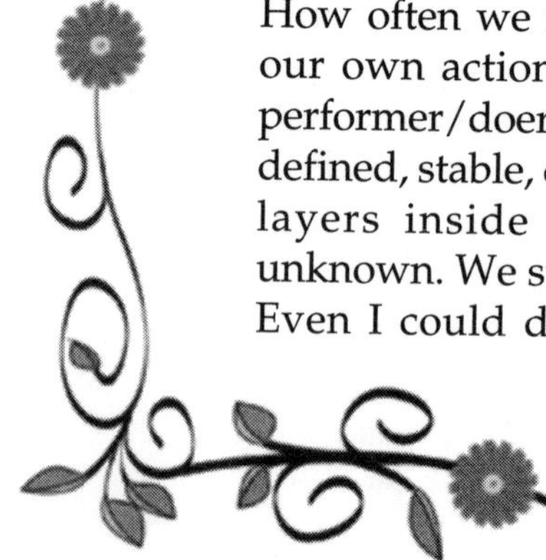

mystery or that inexplicable occurrence makes life a poem, not a mathematical theorem.

Yes, my students, I know you are reading. You are reading how Durkheim interpreted the totemic symbol, how Weber interpreted the Calvinist doctrine of predestination, how Clifford Geertz interpreted the Balinese cock fight. You are reading about Dilthey's 'transposition', Gadamer's 'fusion of horizons'. But then, never forget that it is not a technique, not just a methodological skill; understanding is life itself. Live life. Feel life. Touch life. Wonder. Love. Fail. Rise. Make the metamorphosis possible—from technique to poetry, from information to illumination. Your life, believe it, is the embodiment of hermeneutics.

11

Yes, my eyes look at the treasure of printed words stored in *The German Ideology, Economic and Philosophic Manuscripts of 1844* and *Capital*; my brain cognizes, analyzes and dissects this huge bundle of information; my pen creates essays that need the certification of scholarship. But I do something more. With love and pain, with laughter and humour, with dream and aspiration, with sunrise and sunset I engage with Marx. I de-Brahminize Marx.

We—university scholars—are known for our rigorous critique of Brahminism: the way it hierarchizes human faculties and society, its story of degradation of manual labour, its central emphasis on intellectual cognition and abstract knowledge rather than love and action, the way it sanctifies select texts as the ultimate source of knowledge and wisdom, and sees that these texts remain confined to the select elite, and do not get disseminated among people. This critique is immensely significant and powerful. However, I ask myself: What are we doing? Isn't it that we too are practising yet another form of Brahminism—possibly secular, but nevertheless equally hierarchical, textual, esoteric and cognitive? I cannot deny this anxiety; every moment it confronts me. I wish to face it, and maybe this acknowledgement leads to a new awakening and practice.

To begin with, let me reflect on the way we

have grown up in a modern university, the way it has socialized us, trained us and shaped our consciousness. We strive for knowledge, for some sort of abstract theorization to make sense of the world. Disembodied intellect, pure cognition, discursive reasoning, abstract thought—these are some of our distinctive markers. We think. We theorize. We philosophize. We debunk. We critique. But seldom do we engage ourselves in practice; it is like erecting a wall: the abstraction/purity of thought should by no means be contaminated by practice, by everydayness, by hands and legs. We have already hierarchized our faculties, and thereby people around us. We feel we are superior because we think and theorize; and others are just 'workers' engaged in mundane activities of the world! Not solely that. We also give excessive importance to select texts as the ultimate source of knowledge and wisdom. To be a university scholar is to sanctify these texts, legitimate one's being, one's every word, one's gesture through these texts. So *Manusmriti*, *Upanishads* and the *Bhagavad Gita* are now replaced by another set of texts: say, Emile Durkheim's *The Rules of Sociological Method*, Karl Marx's *Capital* or Michel Foucault's *The Archaeology of Knowledge*. But the attitude remains the same. To know the world is to know these texts; and those who can't master these texts are, therefore, not truly knowledgeable; their sense of the world is bound to be inferior!

Moreover, it is to be seen that these texts remain 'sacred'; no dilution should be allowed; no contamination should be permitted to 'pollute' their purity; and hence their popularization, it is thought, is dangerous. Sanskrit is replaced by contemporary academic vocabulary—its heavily loaded and mystified language. Not to speak this language is to miss the rigour of academics!

We continue to engage in this practice. Yet, how paradoxical it is that we call ourselves anti-Brahminical! The fact is that we too are Brahmins—modern/secular/academic Brahmins. I have a sense of discomfort. And out of this discomfort emerges my quest, my search for a new practice of learning. Yes, I am aware that I can be misunderstood. It is possible to allege that I am devaluing these texts; I am bringing the emotive elements of love, poetry and action in a domain that is supposed to be absolutely textual, intellectual and theoretical. And hence I am popularizing or diluting the seriousness of these texts. But as a teacher I need to make my position clear. I am by no means against these texts. I read the *Upanishads*; I read Marx and Durkheim. I read the *Bhagavad Gita*; I read Foucault and Habermas. I read theology, Sufi tales and Puranic narratives; I read about poststructuralism, postcolonialism and postmodernism. But then, no matter how important these texts are, my experience of the world through the movement of my hands and

legs, my feeling, my love, my practice are no less important. In fact, it is the richness of my being that helps me to have a conversation with these texts and disseminate in a language that is mine, that is deep and authentic—not borrowed, ornamental and esoteric. And I keep telling my students: read, read these texts, but not even for a second think that your labour, your pain, your love and your historicity are unimportant. Each of us must rediscover, feel, interpret and engage with these texts in unique ways.

Friends, that is why, I do not feel very easy with all these 'orientation programmes' that seek to train, condition and dictate: How to read Marx, how to read Foucault, how to write a thesis, how to write a book review, how to write a research paper. This 'how' business, I am afraid, is Brahminical; it imposes the expertized opinion (or the opinion of the academic priest craft) on you; it devalues you. As a result, it leads to ruthless homogenization. Like a trained dog, everyone seeks to repeat the same jargon, quote the same text, follow the same style. It looks like a manufactured product; it loses its fragrance, its soul. It is ritualistic. In our seminars and conferences we keep reciting the *mantras* of these rituals.

Yes, friends, let me tell you my own story. I read Karl Marx not just through my 'intellect' and 'cognitive power'; I read Marx not just in a sanitized library, in a seminar hall amidst

experts. I read Marx as I visit a mall—the magical/surgical space that global capitalism has created, see the spectacular display of goods and commodities and look at their mythologies; I read Marx as I see the power of credit card—its instantaneity that stimulates the urge to consume, possess and define one's essence in terms of the vicarious pleasure of consumption. I find my Marx. I understand 'commodity fetishism'; I understand 'alienation'; I understand the 'power of money'. In fact, I read Marx through love, through pain, through anger, through dream. Yes, my eyes look at the treasure of printed words stored in *The German Ideology, Economic and Philosophic Manuscripts of 1844* and *Capital*; my brain cognizes, analyzes and dissects this huge bundle of information; my pen creates essays that need the certification of scholarship. But I do something more. With love and pain, with laughter and humour, with dream and aspiration, with sunrise and sunset I engage with Marx. I de-Brahminize Marx.

And dear students, I want you to find your Marx, your Foucault, your Simone de Beauvoir in your own way—through your unique journey, through your intellect, experience, hope, disillusionment, love and pain. I don't think that because of this these texts get trivialized. Instead, the texts acquire a soul, and become intimate and experiential. And only then is it possible to communicate authentically, to free these texts from the monopoly of

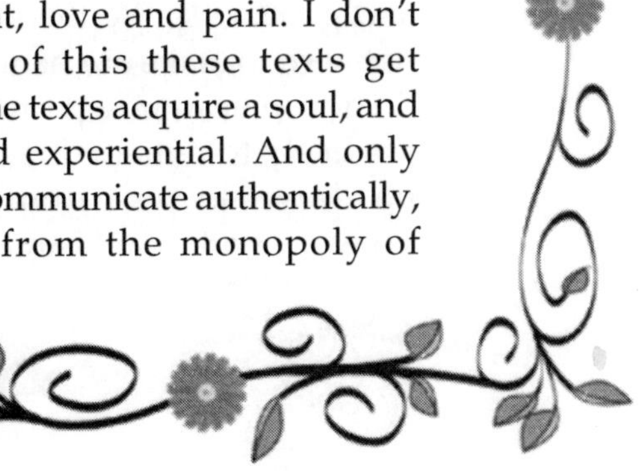

modern/secular Brahmins—our university scholars. You need not cause an obstacle by speaking a mystified/ difficult/esoteric language. We know how through simple, yet revealing tales Ramakrishna could communicate what a 'knowledgeable' scholar (a Brahmin pandit who has just read the scriptures, but failed to experience the light of truth) could not. Kabir could narrate what the institutionalized priest craft could not. And Tagore could write extraordinarily illuminating essays without footnotes and references. This is possible only when love, experience and practice become as important as intellectual cognition. Our academic culture needs its Ramakrishna, Kabir and Tagore to de-scriptualize and de-Brahminize it.

It is sad that we remain indifferent to such a possibility. And its consequences are devastating. For example, we theorize: Can the subaltern speak? But for most of us, it is so difficult to initiate a simple/ non-pretentious conversation with a peasant, a rickshaw puller, a coolie, a vendor, a barber; we fail to realize that they too are people like us; they too love, feel, become angry; they too have envy, jealousy and good will. We theorize labour. But we do not wish to make our hands dirty. So if sweepers do not come, our department rooms and toilets are likely to remain dirty; if peons are on leave no file would move from one corner to another. To work with hands and legs is the experience of a 'worker', and hence unimportant in the domain of knowledge. To feel, to love, to relate is the experience of a poet, and hence unimportant in the making of theories. Friends, that is our secular Brahminism. We ought to overcome it. Believe it, knowledge, love and action, or for that matter, theory and poetry are inseparable. When they are merged, a new being is born—not hierarchical, but essentially integral, communicative and wholistic. And then you read Marx, and you love people, feel their pain, and seek to merge with them. You read feminist theories. And you converse with thousands of ordinary women; with your love and practice you begin to heal them. You read Talcott Parsons; but you do not hesitate to have a cup of tea with the security guard in your university, listen to his narratives, and examine whether the Parsonian grand 'social system' can really accommodate the agony of the security guard. You read Gandhi, and you feel encouraged to experiment with your body, and feel the power of fasting. You no longer remain just a 'knowledgeable' scholar burdened with books, with information, with inflated egos getting dirty, cold and cynical; instead, you are reborn. You become a lover, a bhakta, a worker. Your knowledge acquires its soul; science becomes poetry; information becomes awakening; theory becomes experiential; texts become life's blood. You begin to radiate the waves of love, humility and positivity. That is

your religiosity. And true religiosity is always anti-Brahminical. Dear students, if there is any gift I wish to give you, it is precisely this religiosity.

12

The act of teaching/writing is inherently creative; it needs its own rhythm, own moments of intense engagement, contemplation and silence; and when you deny it, treat it as an instant product, a measurable commodity, ideas are bound to suffer.

One thing I have always loved to imagine is that a teacher's life is peaceful. He/she is not in a hurry; reading great books, arousing the imagination of young minds, transforming the classroom into a sacred space, and radiating the waves of positive energy—a teacher, I have imagined, lives meaningfully and gracefully. No competitiveness. No restlessness. Only calmness and immense energy in the finest pedagogic act of sharing and disseminating ideas, visions, theories and practices. I know that I fail. Yet, the ideal has not ceased to exist; from the valley I see the peak; I see its beauty; I seek my inspiration from it.

However, as I see the world, interact with my colleagues, meet new/young teachers, I feel that something is changing. There is restlessness; competitiveness is everywhere; there seems to be no peace inside; there is a constant urge to produce, to perform, to

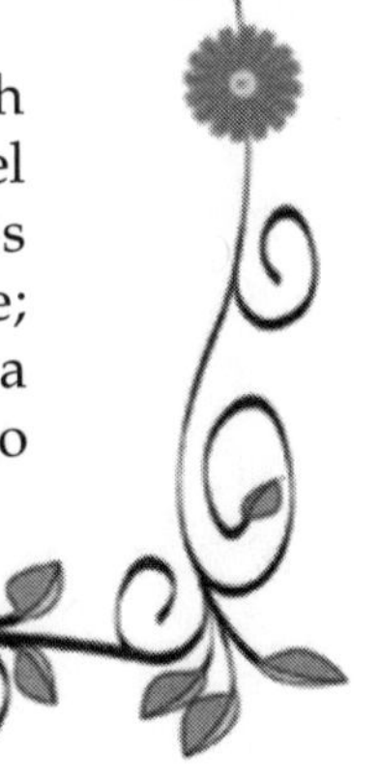

demonstrate, to measure and quantify one's achievements. How many books have you published? How many research papers have you written? How many conferences/seminars have you attended? How many projects have you undertaken? Friends, believe me, it is war... constant war, a reckless race. It seems to be an enactment of a play leading to the survival of the fittest. Why is it happening? An immediate reason is that universities are measuring the qualities of an academic in terms of an absurd scale. Beneath it, it seems, there is a belief that everything has to be measured, nothing exists beyond the scope of quantification, and hence what is immeasurable is immaterial or insignificant. Suppose you are a good thinker. You read great books. You reflect. You work hard to invite your students to the world of ideas. And you love its beauty, its silence, its rhythm. You love this experience because it is immeasurable. But then in the age of numbers you are led to believe that you are nothing if a statistician can't measure the number of seminars you have attended, the number of sessions you have chaired, or the numbers of books/papers you have published. Your contemplation is your fault; your willingness to avoid this fast track, this rat race is your stupidity—your inability to write and prove! Your promotion, your position in the academic hierarchy—everything depends on your 'score': the mythical number of success.

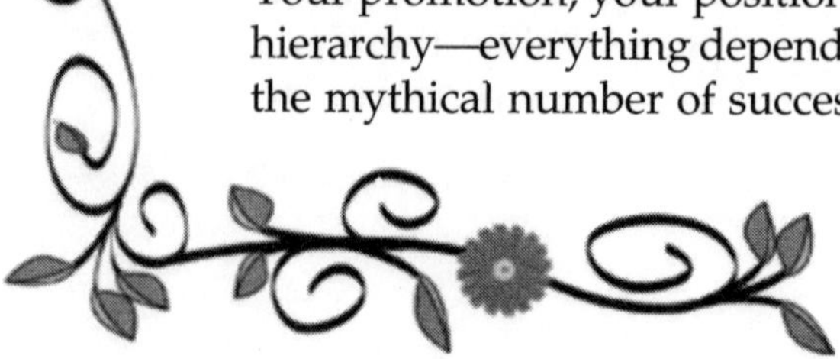

It is, therefore, not surprising if my young colleagues ask me: 'Sir, tell me the number of articles we have to write or the conferences we have to attend or the certificates we have to demonstrate as the proof of our participation in international seminars in order to be eligible for Associate Professorship.' Writing desperately, producing papers in all sorts of conferences, trying to attend any conference in Europe/America, paying a huge registration fee for attending such conferences, or paying money to the publication house for bringing out a book which has to be shown before the selection committee—all these practices which acquire yet another meaning in an essentially corrupt society like ours make the mind perplexed, restless and aggressive. See its damaging consequences. No great work is done when you are in a hurry. Moreover, the act of teaching/writing is inherently creative; it needs its own rhythm, own moments of intense engagement, contemplation and silence; and when you deny it, treat it as an instant product, a measurable commodity, ideas are bound to suffer. True, books are written, edited volumes are published, seminars—national and international—are held, and new journals keep coming. Yet, beneath this 'academic activism' there is a great loss. There is no spontaneity; there is no joy in reading and writing; there is no peace; there is no excitement for coming to the class, meeting young minds, discussing a

book, an idea, a theory, and celebrating it without any anxiety whether it can be measured, or whether it can lead to a paper, a deliberation in an international conference. Our finest moments of joy are non-utilitarian; there is no profit, no loss. But it is sad that today everything ought to have its utility. It generates immense anxiety. I can, therefore, understand what my student who is now teaching in a newly formed central university means when he says: 'Sir, I love teaching. I love my students. I read a great deal for every lecture I deliver. But I haven't published much. What will happen to me, Sir?'

I meet them. They come. They articulate their anguish. I do not know whether I can advise them. Who am I to do that? However, I feel deep pain. At times, I tell them: 'Live peacefully. Don't be in a race. Keep growing as a teacher. Read. Reflect. Celebrate. Write when there is a call, when there is something you wish to communicate with all intensity and conviction. Don't disturb your own rhythm. Surrender yourself before this rhythm. Everything else will be taken care of.' It is difficult, I know. The 'system' wants them to become restless and competitive; their 'career' depends on their 'measurable' performance. And at a time when because of the general decline in the quality of higher education and corrupt university administration there is no trust, the mechanism of 'quality control' assumes this absurd dimension. But the tragedy is that while it promotes the 'smart' players to prove their worth through all sorts of academic products (when numbers alone matter, who is bothering about quality?), it demoralizes those who are honest and authentic, who love to work—and work creatively—in their own rhythm. That is the ultimate irony.

I begin to look at myself. Am I free from this pressure, this tyranny of numbers? Possibly my location is different. With grey hair and years of experience, I can say 'no' to many of these practices; but, I admit, it is not so easy for young minds who have just joined the vocation. Yet, it should not be forgotten that I too experienced immense pressure. However, my faith, my ideal, my priorities, my inner voice helped me. It was not easy. Even now I keep working on myself in order to retain my sanity. Yes, I have written books; but these books have emerged out of pain, dream, longing; my books serve my existential need; I do not know whether they fit into what the academic bureaucracy regards as 'useful' production. I have attended seminars and conferences; but I keep no record because, more often than not, I laugh at this play of words. I play and then I forget. I do not carry it. My bio-data is empty. They ask me: 'Why don't you go abroad?' I teach in a leading university; almost all my colleagues go abroad quite frequently; I am expected to follow the same practice; that is the

pressure. Yes, I wish to see the world as a wanderer; I wish to see its people, its cultures, its rivers, forests, mountains, seas, deserts, islands. But I have now acquired the courage to question the fetish—'There is no other way. You have to go abroad if you are a good academic.' To my mind, this is slavery—a symptom of our colonized consciousness, our failure to believe in our own worth, our inability to differ and create our own reference point. I know that it is not easy to live like this, particularly when everyone around you—your students, your colleagues, your friends, your relatives—begin to see you as somewhat 'abnormal'. Yet, I seek to live on my own terms, and I am happy about it.

'Why don't you have your books published by an international publication house?'—the question confronts me; colleagues ask me, students ask me. I remain silent. Or, I laugh. I feel that even people like us can't avoid the temptation of 'brand' names. It is a 'brand' publication house that defines you, the substance of your book. What you write is not so important; what acquires importance is the name of the publication house. What else is it other than academic consumerism? Your 'prestige' rests on the 'brands' you consume. I differ. I believe that if your book is meaningful, if your writings emanate from the authenticity of your being, even an 'unknown' publishing house—provided it is sincere in its endeavour,

and does its work with a reasonable degree of technical/professional perfection—would take your book to the reader; it would be read, sold, reviewed and discussed. You need to believe in yourself. Why is it—I ask myself—that we become excessively 'brand conscious'? Why is it that we lose faith in ourselves? Why is it that we are perpetually restless for acquiring a 'name'—a foreign university, an international publication and so on and so forth? I fight my battle. I choose to live without these ornaments. I have made a choice. It makes me light. It frees me from the trap of never-ending insecurity and restlessness.

I can imagine what the new generation is facing. I can imagine their anxiety, restlessness and ambivalence. I do not know whether I have an answer to their questions. But then, I can pray; I can express my good will; I can share my stories, my failure, my efforts. As I see myself in a world characterized by reckless competition and restlessness, I feel that I am still fortunate. I am in a vocation that continues to give me calmness, peace and creative freedom. I do not wish to lose it. Why should I lose it in the name of 'success'? What I receive is immeasurable. Why should I always think in terms of concrete/tangible numbers? I recall a very memorable semester. I taught a course on sociological theory. For six months I lived with theory; I breathed theory; and I sought to communicate it in a manner so that my young

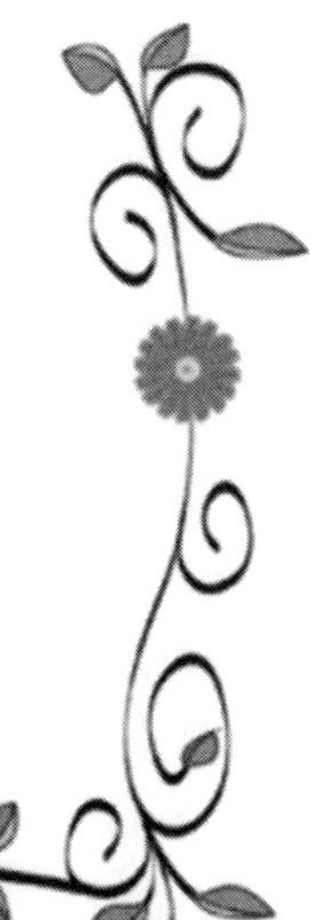

students overcome 'theory phobia', and experience the rhythmic connectedness between theory and lived reality. Every moment, for me, was a celebration; I loved to play with pedagogy and theory. Yes, I could have written a research paper in a trendy journal on the modes of teaching theory. Or, I could have attended a couple of conferences, and delivered lectures on theory and pedagogy. But I did nothing of the sort. No publication, no conference; yet, so much learning and inner development! Those who love numbers would conclude that in that semester I did nothing. But those who have not yet lost their sanity would realize that what I gained was immeasurable. Yes, I evolved as a teacher; and my understanding of sociological theories acquired a new meaning.

Dear students, in your eyes I wish to see that calmness, that peace, that depth which I have always idealized. I trust you. And hence I acquire the courage to tell you a story, a fairy tale. It is midnight. I have studied. I have listened to music. I have thought, reflected and prepared my lecture. And I have just come to my balcony. I look at the sky. I see a star. I see you. I pray. And I feel immensely happy that tomorrow my lecture would be a gift to you: a gift of positive energy and good will. I enter the domain of the immeasurable. I realize the poetry of my vocation. Al that is 'official' and measurable—number of publications,

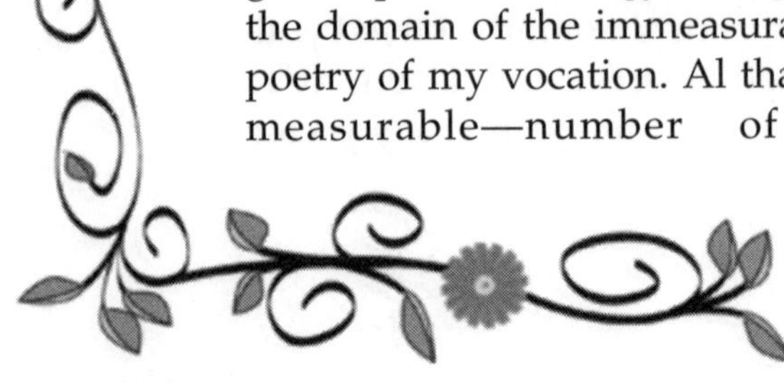

conferences, edited volumes, projects, positions in academic bodies and committees—seems utterly superficial. What remains is just a longing: a teacher walking with his students, and watching the eternity of sunrise and sunset.

13

Life becomes my book; a living engagement with nature becomes my inspiration; and my notion of being an academic undergoes a dramatic transformation. I do not conquer. I relate. I am not just a specialist. I become a lover of life. My pen becomes my brush, my intellect becomes my colour, my awareness becomes my canvas, my teaching/learning/ writing becomes my painting.

I have borrowed a book from one of my students. He loved the book, and wanted me to read it. It is a wonderful book entitled *Being a University* written by Ronald Barnett. Here is a book that reveals the subtle consciousness of an educationist: his sharp reflections on the state of higher education—the way universities all over the world are fast becoming instrumental, losing mysteries, wonder and deep philosophy, and the way in the name of 'useful' research and market demands universities are becoming 'entrepreneurial'. True, there is rapid progress in knowledge-production, there is 'efficiency', and there is reckless competition for 'world ranking'. Yet, there is something fundamental we seem to be missing: our quest for a meaning, for love, for care, for connectedness with the world. And it is in this context that the author constructs his utopia: his plea that it is the right time to strive for an 'ecological' university—a university that seeks to restore all that we have lost, a university that cares, a university that makes us sensitive, humane and deeply ethical/ spiritual.

The book moves me. However, one question confronts me: Why is it that my young student loves the book? And why is it that he intends to write his PhD thesis on an issue having a similar concern: how the ethos of marketization in the neo-liberal era is altering the character of our universities—the way we define ourselves as teachers and researchers, or the way we legitimate certain branches of knowledge and devalue others? Possibly my student has refused to become 'pragmatic'; he retains his dream. Possibly he feels that it is high time we began to restore humanness and moral sensibilities in our universities, and appreciate a domain which exists beyond what the market captures. Possibly he feels that only then can we move towards love, care, mystery, connectedness and what the author of the book regards as an 'ecological university'.

My student's dream fascinates me. And it arouses hope in human possibilities. He comes from a modest background; society must be telling him that he needs money, he needs a job or what these days we regard as a 'placement with a lucrative package', he needs to survive; he too would be asked to marry, to settle down, to buy a car, an apartment, to take his family to Dubai or Singapore for a vacation. He is not

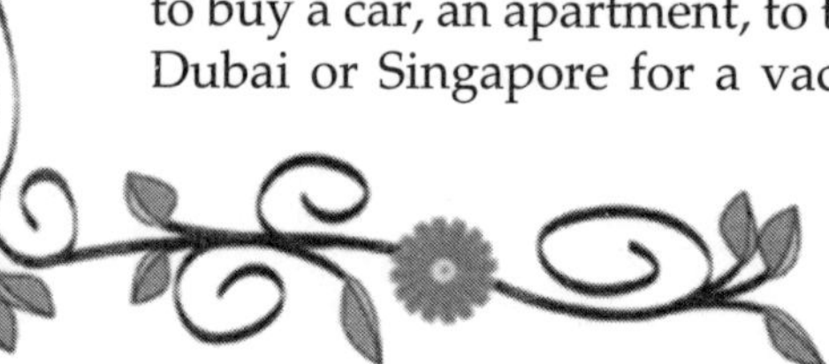

naïve. He knows the world. He knows that ideals do not fill one's stomach. He knows that Tagore or Barnett would not provide him with a job. He knows that a course in information technology or management studies is a more 'guaranteed' road to 'success' in life. He knows that for many a technical job assures survival, and it is more important than a philosophic reflection. He knows that it is absurd to imagine everyone pursuing liberal/humanistic education. He knows that it is not easy to overcome the 'constraint' of the Durkheimian 'social fact'. He knows that the emerging private universities—with their 'market-friendly' courses—are becoming the order of the day because the aspiring middle class wants 'success' and quick results, and sees no other alternative to neo-liberalism and its 'pragmatic' discourses on education. He knows; he is intelligent enough to know all these hard facts of existence. Yet, he dreams; he seems to have a mission; he does not wish to write just another 'value- neutral' PhD thesis; he seeks to inject his mission, dreams and utopias into it.

And I am moved. I realize once again that it is wonderful to be a teacher. Your students—not necessarily always your colleagues—illumine your being. It is sad that many of us, despite our secure jobs and academic locations, are not in a position to speak the language that my student wishes to utter. Possibly we are becoming too pragmatic. Knowledge, we tend

to think, ought to be produced as a 'product'. Our research, our publications, our projects must sell. At a time when because of this survival anxiety in the domain of market-driven academics we are depriving ourselves of poetry, mystery and wonder, my student comes as a refreshing departure. And possibly an association with students like him makes me move, experiment, and do things which, I am afraid, my 'pragmatic' colleagues may not always appreciate. How often I tell my students that a university is a place for celebration. Learning is celebration; teaching is celebration; studentship is celebration. A university need not be seen as just a 'serious' place without laughter, without music, without colours, without festivals, without dreams. A university need not be seen as just a place that trains one for a lucrative/professional job. A university, I keep telling my students, is a celebration of life. As I see my university, I feel that it is also about its trees that whisper in my ears, its flowers that make me see the beauty of illumination in silence, its curved paths that wait for a mystical embrace with the full moon night, its birds that give a melancholic meaning to the colourful sky at the time of sunset. I learn from my long walk, from those tiny butterflies which soften my intellect, from the old woman who touches my head and blesses me, from an old man and his wife who come every morning from a neighbouring locality to feed the animals. Life becomes my book; a living engagement with nature becomes my inspiration; and my notion of being an academic undergoes a dramatic transformation. I do not conquer. I relate. I am not just a specialist. I become a lover of life. My pen becomes my brush, my intellect becomes my colour, my awareness becomes my canvas, my teaching/learning/writing becomes my painting.

I, therefore, dare. I ask my students to celebrate the entire process of learning. I ask them to travel, to see places, to connect with people (irrespective of 'field work'), to communicate, to see films, to listen to good music, to read great biographies, to draw beautiful sketches, to create colourful wall magazines, to decorate the classroom with flowers, to take a camera, to move around the campus, explore the natural beauty of the campus and make a documentary film. I ask them to arouse their potential, to realize that they are not just 'resources' for the nation's economic growth; they are essentially poets, singers, dancers, writers, lovers of nature. I ask them to believe that they are creating a sane culture: a culture that defies the colonization of what the market-driven culture industry dictates—loud music, noise, meaningless speed, inner void amidst outer glamour. I do not know whether I succeed. Possibly not. Yet, the book that my student loves, and gives me to read makes me believe that I ought to try. To fail is

not your tragedy; to give up is your ultimate fall. So I tell them; 'Don't mind even if it does not count in your bio-data. Don't mind even if it is not useful for 'world ranking'. Don't mind even if some of your professors refuse to acknowledge or appreciate your effort. But realize that you are finding yourself. You are giving life, mystery, colour, beauty, connectedness to a university. You are trying to make it ecological'.

Life goes on. It surprises. I find a letter from one of my students:

> *I hardly dream during daytime sleep.... I don't, but this afternoon I did. And surprisingly I also remember it. I saw the 'sea'. Yes, I have never visited one and this afternoon I dreamt of it. It was so blue and slightly greenish.... I could even see colours in my dream, there is a rose occurrence. I would often imagine myself standing on top of a cliff, and I am wearing white loose clothes, the wind brushing against me and the sound of the waves....Oh so beautiful....Of course that is something which has not happened yet, but I imagine and this time in my dream I saw it and I saw myself jumping from the cliff to the water....I didn't seem to be scared of the sea....I was swimming and swimming and then suddenly I was back on top of the cliff...*

Your dream, my dear, is a beautiful gift. What else does a teacher want? You keep me alive. My university touches the sea, the cliff...

14

A teacher carries a lamp: a small, beautiful lamp. Its light softens one's heart, illumines one's being; it is not gorgeous because all that is gorgeous is noisy and pretentious; what is beautiful is simple and unassuming. And hence a classroom where a teacher is engaged in a deep communion with his students is the abode of God.

I think. I read. I contemplate. I come to my class, deliver a lecture, engage with my students, seek to arouse their imagination, and open the windows of their minds. What else can a teacher do? Here is a teacher: simple and unknown. Here is a teacher engaged in an art that is neither big nor spectacular. No 24*7 live coverage; something non-glamorous is happening in silence—a teacher interacts with a group of students. Meanwhile, the world—the 'real' world—is showing its theatrical play, displaying its packages, its mythologies. There are leaders, and they are promising 'development'; television channels are projecting them as ad products; people are voting, getting carried away by the 'wave'; the mantra of success is proclaimed loudly. And the leader, it is declared, has finally arrived; he is strong and assertive; he means business; he delivers! At times, I find myself completely irrelevant and insignificant in a noisy environment of this kind. I find myself as a stranger in this landscape. What then do I do as a teacher? Is my art relevant any more? Does it make any difference? These are difficult questions; I keep thinking, reflecting, contemplating.

Television doesn't fascinate me much. Yet, at times, with a remote in my hand I pass through innumerable channels. I see the glorification of the trivia. Television news readers—they are smart, English-speaking, good looking; yet, beneath these externalities (glamour, instant stardom, narcissism) there is absolute superficiality. Seldom does one see a serious engagement with an issue, a sincere effort to understand what we are passing through—acute poverty amidst vulgar affluence; express highways, flyovers, malls, multiplexes amidst lack of basic facilities for a large section of people; exclusive international schools and private universities amidst poor quality government schools; growth rate and IPL amidst hunger and malnutrition. Yes, development becomes a myth. It is an external decorum seeking to hide the dark interior. Development becomes a playground for corporate capitalism, for real estate mafias, for the aspiring consumptionist middle class. Its hardness manifests itself in the mantra of unlimited desire, competitiveness and recklessness. Television anchors celebrate it;

they invite their chosen 'experts'; they generate noise. And we keep consuming it. See the cultural landscape. Television serials are loud; music is loud; ads are loud. There is only one message—consume everything, consume food, consume cars, consume bullet trains, consume bank loans, consume property, consume happiness, consume nirvana and salvation, consume mountains, deserts, oceans, consume sex, consume pleasure. This principle of consumption is inherently aggressive and intolerant. It abhors softness, simplicity, poetry and depth. Television news, everyday political discourses, soap operas, loud music, express highways, speedy cars and drunk driving, gated communities, multiplexes, malls—all are deeply related and connected.

And, as the heart of a teacher whispers, everything is related to education—the kind of education that is seen as 'useful', 'productive' and 'success-oriented'. Imagine the fate of a schoolchild. As she completes Standard VIII, her 'coaching' begins; innumerable education shops exist to train her, discipline her, prepare her for quick, smart, correct answers that medical/engineering/management institutions would demand in their entrance tests. This drilling, or this ruthless exercise deprives the experience of education of any feeling of joy, contemplation, plurality of ideas, deeper domains of life. The fetish of objective/multiple choice tests kills the spirit of creative learning.

The mind becomes 'efficient', yet dull. It 'solves' problems; but it cannot enter the domain of creativity, imagination and reflexivity. It is violent, ruthless, one-dimensional. This sort of education is devoid of art. There is no music, no prayer, no time to see the sky. Einstein's creativity doesn't exist in such a world; Tagore is a waste of time; Whitman is irrelevant. Creative articulations are not needed; ambiguities are discouraged; contemplative moments for inner growth are prohibited. What matters is the cultivation of 'objective reasoning' that identifies *one and only one* 'correct' answer—quickly, efficiently, smartly. And see the basic driving force beneath this sort of education. It is 'success'—success at any cost; and success is a measurable commodity—it is your salary package, your dowry rate. It begins with schools; it gains its peak in technical institutions; and it culminates into the creation of a 'product': an engineering/management graduate who knows only 'success', who earns, who seeks to earn more, who loathes whatever does not fit into his restricted vision of the world, who is finished from inside.

No wonder, there is no critical thought. You can be violent. You can be instrumental in the mass annihilation of people. You can spread poison for your political victory. You can be restless, totalitarian. But everything is forgotten. Because you promise development! That is the only correct answer; everything else is an ideological fluctuation! Likewise, our 'brightest' young minds can forget everything: poetry, wonder, music, life's mystery so long as a 'placement with an attractive package' is assured. And the aspiring middle class can forget everything—communal violence, naked injustice, poverty, malnutrition, so long as they can drive their cars on smooth express highways, visit malls and multiplexes, find 24-hour water and electricity supply in their fortified housing societies. Authoritarianism comes out of this constant interplay of militant nationalist discourse, aggression of development, bombardment of culture industry, and above all, a system of education that has lost its poetry and metaphysics. And the irony of our times is that democracy legitimates it, people's choices make it sacrosanct, education experts add to its use value, and the media-market alliance causes some sort of *maya* which becomes exceedingly difficult to escape.

Who am I as a teacher in such an environment? It appears that I am nothing; I am irrelevant. I tend to fall down; I begin to crumble. Yet, there is something that keeps me alive. I hear the voice of the ancient sage: *avidya* is darkness; it causes *maya*, arrogance, pride, violence; it is *vidya*—an awakening of the spirit that takes us from the unreal to the real. I acquire the courage to realize—and realize once again—that truth is not propaganda, music is not noise,

development is not aggression, meaningful living is not narcissism, and education is not technical efficiency. I realize that the task of a teacher is to continue this search, this urge to speak of light, even if the mob outside is intoxicated and hypnotized. I become aware of the *swadharma* of a teacher. A teacher carries a lamp: a small, beautiful lamp; its light softens one's heart, illumines one's being; it is not gorgeous because all that is gorgeous is noisy and pretentious; what is beautiful is simple and unassuming. And hence a classroom where a teacher is engaged in a deep communion with his students is the abode of God. It generates the waves of love, reciprocity, plurality, empathy, sensitivity and understanding. It is dialogic. It defies authoritarianism. It is musical. It is poetic. It is spiritual. True, the epic battle does not end; the forces of untruth strike with all sorts of spectacular weapons: media-induced hallucinations and narratives of mega professors with huge fund-generating projects in a networking society. Will the truth survive? You cannot remain a teacher unless you keep carrying the lamp of truth, no matter how hostile the circumstances are.

As I pass through this emotional churning, a student arrives. The violence, the propaganda machinery and the loudness all around seem to have disturbed her. 'Sir, what are you thinking? What is going to happen?' I see a great quest in her eyes. I take her to my garden, and

give her a lemon, a mango: two wonderful gifts from nature. I touch her head, bless her: 'My dear, truth is this simple act, this act of prayer and offering. So long as we have the sensitivity to celebrate this beauty, there is hope. Take the lamp from me. I wish to follow you.'

15

Education, it ought to be realized, is about the cultivation of a mind that sees the infinite in the finite. Tagore was born in Bengal. You are a Maharashtrian; yet, you can engage with Tagore because deep poetry transcends barriers. I am not a Dalit. Yet, I can study Ambedkar because a libertarian urge is also my urge. Education is about overcoming these constraining identity markers and associated barriers; it is a quest for the universal.

How often I realize that teaching a course is not just about completing the syllabus, and evaluating the assignments of students. With every course you teach you are reborn. You grow—intellectually, ethically and spiritually. It is this perpetual evolution towards a higher centre of being that transforms one's pedagogy into an aesthetic play. Difficulties come, obstacles confront you, and as a teacher you realize that with these difficulties, resistances and challenges you grow. Possibly, as every seeker feels, difficulties become your blessings. I have taught many courses. However, one course that I have found most difficult and challenging to pursue is called *Modern Indian Social Thought*. Emotive outbursts and passions, heated argumentations, conflicting perspectives, ideology and rhetoric, stereotypes and branding: every moment generates turmoil and restlessness. Yet, I need to remain calm, and encourage my students to sharpen the art of listening. I admit that it is not easy; the process is emotionally intense and excessively challenging. But I wish to accept this challenge with absolute humility.

Why is it that this course causes so much passion? One important reason, I believe, is that it is deeply intimate; it is about our own history, our politico-social biographies, our destinies. As I feel, it is possible for a student to reduce Giddens, Habermas and Foucault into an academic puzzle, a fascinating item for cultural capital. True, these thinkers are immensely appealing; but then, their distance from our everydayness reduces the possibility of an extreme form of emotional reaction. However, things acquire a different character when one begins to speak of Vivekananda, Ambedkar and Gandhi. Social identities, political ideologies, religious beliefs, historical memories, everyday gossip, cultural stereotypes: everything emerges as a stumbling block. As a result, one tends to miss the calmness and endurance to go deeper; instead, one hates, one worships, one shouts, one stops others. So for some, Gandhi was simply a Hindu/Gujarati *bania* who was against the interests of the marginalized castes and the working class. For some, Ambedkar was God; there is nothing that can be said to be problematic about him. For some, Indian philosophy is heavily Brahminical, and hence to refer to it in the class is a waste of time and energy. And for some, the course acquires a meaning only when you speak of the Marxian contribution to the making of Indian social thought. See the paradox. When you do a course in Social Theories, you have no problem, you are willing to submit; even if you are a committed Marxist you cannot demand: ' I will study only Karl Marx. I will not study Emile Durkheim or Talcott Parsons.' But the moment something about India is taught, there is impatience, there is always some sort of an identity/stereotype attached to a thinker: 'Oh, Sir speaks of Tagore in the class because he is a Bengali; or, Oh, Sir has delivered three lectures on Jotiba Phule, but only one lecture on Narayana Guru; see his biases, he neglects the South!'

Another difficulty emanates from a largely left-centric ideological milieu prevalent in the campus. As it becomes reductionist and deterministic, one tends to write slogans, and reduce a serious philosophic debate into a mere rhetoric, a stereotype. Hence if you refer to Swami Vivekananda and Vedanta, it is quite likely that you are suspected as a 'rightist'. ' Oh, Sir is quoting the Upanishads in the class. See the hidden curriculum—a Brahminical conspiracy!' We lose patience; we refuse to go deeper; the easy task of labelling comforts us; we miss the subtle beauty of a thinker. Our strong political likes and dislikes disturb the rhythm of a meaningful conversation.

Vivekananda—a Hindu nationalist; Sri Aurobindo—a mere idealist; Tagore—a bhadralok romantic; and a teacher asking his students to study them as seriously as they study Pierre Bourdieu and Jurgen Habermas is certainly deviating from what a progressive university ought to do!

I am growing up with these challenges. There are moments when I too have become excited, lost my temper. I have felt: 'Why am I taking this trouble? It is easy to teach theory, it is safe to speak of Michel Foucault and Levi Strauss. Why am I coming to the class with Gandhi's Experiments, Tagore's religiosity, Sri Aurobindo's path-breaking Uttarpara speech? Why am I allowing myself to be perceived as a philosopher, not an empirical sociologist; a dreamer filled with poetry, not a progressive rationalist with a baggage of political correctness?'Yes, there are moments of doubt. Yet, I rise, close my eyes, and begin to see a series of episodes unfolding before my eyes. I begin to realize that despite all these challenges and resistances, some flowers have bloomed, some new insights have emerged, some stereotypes are broken, and some possibilities have charmed us.

I am introducing Allama Iqbal: a gifted poet-thinker—his evolution, his essays on Islam, politics and culture, his engagement with the Muslim League, his not so easy relationship with Mohammad Ali Jinnah, and his

remarkably brilliant poetry. The class gains its momentum. I refer to some of his poems—the way these poems enrich our sociological imagination, and reveal the poet's sensitivity, his pain, his utopia, his anguish. But then, a student asks: 'Sir, why Iqbal? Why not a Tamil poet, a Telugu poet, a Punjabi poet? Why this special preference for Iqbal?' I feel the question; it is emerging out of a terrible anxiety over 'democratic representation'. India's diversity, heterogeneity, plurality, it is thought, must be adequately and democratically represented in everything I teach. So, as the argument goes, Iqbal can be taught only if all great poets from all Indian languages are taught. Otherwise, to teach Iqbal is to do injustice to others! Is it possible in a course that continues only for a semester? Or, for that matter, is it at all desirable? Is education about voting and a clever strategy for making everyone 'happy'—the way our power-hungry/ambitious politicians visit a Dalit household, organize the Iftar party, and speak broken regional languages while campaigning for elections? Education, it ought to be realized, is about the cultivation of a mind that sees the infinite in the finite. Tagore was born in Bengal. You are a Maharashtrian; yet, you can engage with Tagore because deep poetry transcends barriers. I am not a Dalit. Yet, I can study Ambedkar because a libertarian urge is also my urge. Education is about overcoming these constraining identity

markers and associated barriers; it is a quest for the universal.

As all these thoughts come to my mind, a student rises up. 'Sir, may I say something?' 'Why not? Go ahead', I reply. The young boy from Karnataka smiles, and with absolute calmness makes a revealing statement: 'To understand one great poet is to understand all great poets. To study Iqbal is to become sensitive to the world of poetry—the essence of the poetic imagination. It is enriching, fulfilling.' I feel immensely happy. A symmetry takes place between the teacher and the taught. My student's remarks come as soothing rains after a heavy storm in the class.

Gandhi was bad; Ambedkar was good. Gandhi was a casteist; Ambedkar sought to annihilate caste. Gandhi remained a Hindu; Ambedkar debunked Hinduism. Gandhi was anti-modern, superstitious; Ambedkar was modern and progressive. Gandhi was a reactionary; Ambedkar was a magician with answers to everything. Yes, these stereotypes and superficialities keep spreading even in a university like ours. The reasons are many: assertive identity politics, quick/instant political correctness, and refusal to probe, to go deeper, to see beyond posters and slogans. To speak of Gandhi and Ambedkar in the class, needless to add, is not easy. How easy it is to communicate Emile Durkheim's *Elementary Forms of Religious Life*; how difficult it is to invite young students growing up with scepticism and doubt to Gandhi's engagement with the *Bhagavad Gita*! It is easy to communicate Karl Marx's *The Communist Manifesto*, and the theory of class conflict; it is, however, extremely difficult to invite these young students to Gandhi's art of resistance: how the cultivation of 'soul force' and the process of 'self-purification' play an important role in *satyagraha*, in the act of resistance against untruth. Furthermore, an environment has been created in which it is expected that if you speak of Ambedkar, you have to demolish Gandhi. It is almost like reproducing the script of a standardized Hindi film: if there is a hero, there ought to be a villain! Yet, I come, retain my stamina, and run the risk of being branded as a 'sympathizer' of Gandhi. I refer to Gandhi's engagement with the *Bhagavad Gita* and the *Sermon on the Mount*, I narrate his experiments, and try to make them feel that his practices are more important than his words. I tell them how he learned from John Ruskin, realized the importance of labour, and thereby interrogated the Brahminical principle of 'purity vs. pollution'. I refer to Ambedkar's brilliant essay on Buddha and Marx, how even the 'rationalist' Ambedkar realized the need for changing man's conscience for overcoming the caste system, how he engaged with Buddha's *Dhammapada*, and how Ambedkar too became a man of prayer. I ask them to enquire whether Gandhi's

Bhagavad Gita and Ambedkar's Buddhism are irreconcilable. I ask them to enquire whether in our quest for a just society one's ideas and contributions have to be vehemently denied for the glorification of the other. It is at this juncture that a student comes forward, surprises the proponents of identity politics, chooses to write an essay (while invoking the late scholar Professor Nagraj's contributions), and argues why we have to see beyond the fetishization of Ambedkar and hatred of Gandhi; and how a nuanced philosophy of justice ought to negotiate with both. At that moment, my class acquires a different character—not a party school, not a place for writing pamphlets and slogans, but a creative/dialogic space that encourages us to go deeper, and break stereotypes.

With difficulties and possibilities I too grow. As a teacher I learn the fundamental lesson of calmness. Even if students become impatient and restless, I ought to remain calm; I ought to listen; and slowly and steadily I have to create a pedagogic environment that creates the ground for the art of listening. This calmness—or, the wisdom to receive all sorts of condemnations with a smile—is, I believe, an essential characteristic of a teacher. It is extremely difficult to practise. I fail. I fail when I become terribly upset or angry. Yet, I rise because I believe in the virtue of this journey. Moreover, I learn another important lesson—

criticality is not cynicism; criticality is not nihilistic negativity; instead, criticality is the ability to filter, to accept what is enduring and beautiful, and to reject what has lost its meanings; criticality is the art of possibilities. For example, in a plural society like ours, or in a society that runs the risk of experiencing the tyranny of majoritarianism, Swami Vivekananda's references to the glory of 'Hindu culture' might sound somewhat odd and disturbing; yet, it should not prevent me from coming to the class with a series of lectures Swamiji delivered on 'practical Vedanta': how the realization of fundamental 'oneness' or what is felt as Eternal and Deathless can regenerate us, enable us to overcome our fear, limitedness and inertia, and create the foundation of a new civilization—egalitarian and spiritually enriched. I admit that Jawaharlal Nehru's 'developmental' policies might have its discontents; but it should not prevent me from coming to the class with a copy of *The Discovery of India*, and encourage my students to see how the 'modernist' Nehru was becoming ambivalent, how he was realizing the limitations of his Reason nurtured by Charles Darwin, Karl Marx and Sigmund Freud to understand the continual flow of an old civilization like ours, and how he was seeking to engage with its culture, its epics, its literature, its historical trajectory. The Indian Left may not have made its presence felt significantly in the

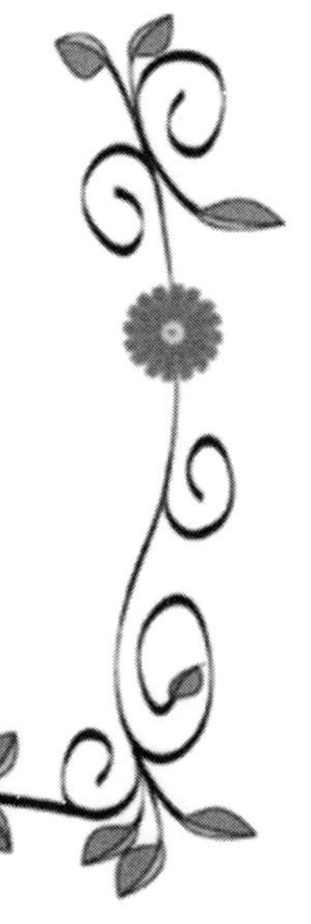

making of our collective imagination. But how can I forget to invite my students to an extraordinary and illuminating life-trajectory of M.N. Roy—his Marxism, his critical engagement with the Communist International, and eventually his radical humanism, his plea for a decentralized partyless democracy?

My criticality has not made me cynical. I have not lost a sense of beauty. And it is indeed a wonderful journey. I tell my students: 'Imagine...imagine you are walking through a dense forest. And you see a marvellous tree called Mohandas Karamchand Gandhi. Have patience. Don't be in a hurry. Sit under the tree. Feel the fragrance, the shade. Undertake a journey with him—towards South Africa, towards Champaran and Dandi, towards Noakhali and Kolkata. But then, you have to move further. Here is yet another magnificent tree called B.R. Ambedkar. Feel his determinism, his ability to overcome all sorts of obstacles, his extraordinary scholarship, his resistance and criticality. Stand up, stand up, friends. It is a huge forest. You have to explore and see. Trees after trees—Sri Aurobindo, Jotiba Phule, Rabindranath Tagore, Allama Iqbal, M.N. Roy. Carry on the journey.'

Yes, I keep walking. And I ask my students to walk. What else is learning except this constant walking? Walking is my ultimate pilgrimage.

16

We are more than what we appear to be. We are the children of the divine, and the divine is boundless. What else is teaching? It is an act of prayer that transforms us. Is the politics of doubt devaluing this prayer, and instead of healing the wound, intensifying it further?

What is so remarkable about the vocation I am engaged in? Oh, I tell myself, my vocation enables me to grow, to expand—not just intellectually, but also ethically and spiritually. I cross boundaries. I overcome all sorts of limiting identities. As every morning I walk towards the university and come to my class, I undergo a process of transformation. I become a teacher. What spreads out from my being is a flow of energy that has no caste, no religion, no gender, no ethnicity. I realize the Universal in me; I realize what unites and connects. In the eyes of my students I see love and wonder, curiosity and eagerness to learn. I do not bother to know their caste, their religion; at the moment of the communion we are all seekers and fellow travellers. How does it matter whether my student is a Bengali or a Tamil, a Muslim or a Christian, a Dalit or a Brahmin? I am a teacher, and they are my students. Nothing else matters. We are learning together, exploring together. And what an extraordinarily liberating feeling it is! I become more than my caste, my religion, my ethnicity, my gender. Even though I speak Bengali, a Tamil student enchants me. I am born in a Hindu family; a Muslim student enters my inner world. I am supposed to be a 'forward caste' intellectual; yet, someone not belonging to my caste makes me realize the sweetness of divinity. All stereotypes crumble. I grow. I realize the beauty of an expanded horizon. It elevates; it does not limit. It expands; it does not restrict. It includes; it does not exclude. Thanks to my vocation; it has helped me to experience what transcends boundaries, to become truly cosmopolitan.

Are we losing this beauty, this grace? There are moments when some sort of anxiety confronts me. I smell a danger. See, for instance, the negative power of caste as one's permanent identity. It divides and separates. It excludes, and limits one's horizon. It erects a wall, and causes doubt and scepticism about others. It sees conspiracy. Yes, caste exists in our society, in our polity. Yes, caste causes atrocities and violence. Yes, even in a university like ours it may not be impossible to find a professor who carries his caste identity. And at a time when social scientists write more and more on caste, when caste-based mobilization and movement—particularly, if it has got a

subaltern touch—is seen as legitimate, when anything universal is seen with doubt and suspicion, and when in an extremely charged political campus like ours not to mention caste is seen as hypocrisy, it is not easy to retain the grace I am talking about. Doubt and mistrust begin to pollute the relationship. Here is a 'Brahmin' professor—he is not very sensitive to the needs of Dalit students, he victimizes them. Or, here is a 'Dalit' professor—see how forward caste students avoid him, and do not want him to be their supervisor! In fact, these days we often hear these whispers, and feel these waves of negativity, doubt and scepticism.

I am not saying that my university is a solitary island, and hence it is free from caste prejudices. But to allow this scepticism to grow, or to begin our educational journey with this doubt is to destroy the basic trust which is needed for a healthy relationship between the teacher and the taught. Yes, we need to be alert. We must fight all sorts of caste prejudice and victimization. But this alertness does not mean that we lose hope. How can higher education evolve if we fail to see the possibility of redemption? My birth, as I feel, is not my final destiny. I may be born in a 'forward caste' family; but my life-philosophies and concrete practices would decide whether I am casteist, or whether I am simply a carrier of the Universal Energy. And as I join the vocation of teaching, I like my students to see this possibility in me; I

like them to see me as just humane—a fellow traveller, a comrade, a being who does not stigmatize the so-called 'backward caste' students; nor does he fix the so-called 'forward caste' students, and make them feel eternally guilty. Instead, I love to see the road ahead; I tell myself and my students: ' We are more than our ascriptive identities. We are more than what we appear to be. We are the children of the divine, and the divine is boundless.' What else is teaching? It is an act of prayer that transforms us. Is the politics of doubt devaluing this prayer, and instead of healing the wound, intensifying it further?

Again, it is unfortunate that we live at a time when a male professor's orientation to a female student is seen with suspicion. True, it is the larger society—its perpetual episodes of male violence, sexual assault, abuse of women—that affects the environment of the university. It is also true that not everyone is capable of living with power; for instance, a supervisor may harass his female PhD student, take advantage of the fact that she is at the receiving end. It is also possible that a professor, despite his scholarship, may not be free from sexual lust, and his sexual gaze might disturb and distort the rhythmic relationship between the teacher and the taught. Again at a time when, thanks to women's initiatives, there is increasing awareness of sexual harassment in workplaces, we see the growing mistrust. The question is how the culture of learning retains its sanity and grace, even when it remains acutely aware of the harsh reality. There is no hope without trust. Imagine how pathetic it would be if we find ourselves in an environment in which a female student feels continually suspicious of her professor's moves, if she feels threatened to come to his chamber, meet him at his residence. Or, how terrible it would be if a male professor becomes extremely apprehensive and laments: 'I am afraid. They can do anything. I am not going to accept any woman as my PhD student.' Or, how crude it is when male students keep spreading rumours: 'See this professor. He favours good looking girls. He gives them good grades.' It is slow poisoning. It does not help. It pollutes the environment further. We have to trust ourselves.

One thing I myself have realized through my teaching engagement is that it is one of the most beautiful/graceful relationships one can think of. My horizon expands. I see immensely bright women. Their scholarship, their struggles, their cultural sensitivity and their spirit of hard work enrich my consciousness. I redefine womanhood. This bond has its beauty, grace and dignity. It takes the relationship to a higher domain filled with boundless affections, blessings and songs of prayer. Sexual exploitation, objectification, lust and greed become impossible. What remains is just poetry. And what else is life-affirming education except

the celebration of poetry?

Yes, I am aware of the fact that the life of a teacher I idealize or seek to experience need not be generalized. My aspirations may be ridiculed, and seen as, to use Dostoyevsky's expressions, 'the dream of a ridiculous man.' Teachers, it may be said, are not from a different planet; they are not with any lofty mission; like any other group of professionals they are doing their job and earning money; and they carry the entire baggage of societal vices: caste prejudice and patriarchal violence. It may also be argued that the age of innocence never existed. And we live at a time when nothing can be trusted, and hence the need of the hour is to intensify the machinery of perpetual doubt, surveillance and legal/disciplinary measures. Committees are formed, posters are written, students conduct protest marches, enquiry commissions are constituted, and an environment is created in which students doubt the integrity of their teachers, and teachers begin to fear their students. Trust disappears; spontaneity withers away. Can a university function like this? Yet, even at the risk of being regarded as 'unreal', I continue to hope. I cannot function with fear and mistrust. I seek to live and function in the way my heart dictates. I invite my students to my residence. I share a cup of coffee and poetry with them. I ask them to come with me and discover the magical landscape of the university on a full moon night. Photography, cinema,

music, art, philosophy—there seems to be no end to this flow of communication. Is it possible that one day I too may be accused as a notorious 'forward caste/ male professor' with all sorts of pathologies? Who knows? I don't bother. I live. I listen to my inner voice. I keep travelling with my students—as a teacher, as a friend, as a potential colleague, as a seeker, as a father. Meanwhile, they come. Someone knocks on my door, and surprises me with beautiful flowers as a gift of gratitude; someone sends a message: 'Sir, it is raining. It seems you are inspired; you must be thinking of your next lecture.' Someone comes forward, her words emanate from eternity; 'Sir, you have just delivered a lecture. Let me bring you a cup of coffee.' It goes on. With sociology and spirituality, with poetry and music, with flowers and books, with mountains and rivers the teacher and the taught become one. Love conquers fear, my dear.

17

It is important to remember that when the burden of 'knowledge' destroys the child within us, some terrible damage to our inner selves takes place. To live with children, to communicate with them, to enchant them, and to be enchanted by them—I believe—is the ultimate strength of a teacher.

Schools continue to fascinate me. My location in a leading university, or my 'status' as a professor has never prevented me from taking an active interest in school education. I do not hierarchize. I do not subscribe to a dualistic division: 'knowledgeable/research-oriented' university professors engaging with serious epistemological issues vs. school teachers merely imparting the lessons of elementary physics, mathematics and language to young children. Instead, I feel a sense of connectedness with schools, with children. Possibly I have never become an 'adult'; I remain a child. I love children's books; at the high altitude of the mountains as I see schoolchildren walking towards their school, I feel I am witnessing divinity; they look as beautiful as the mountains, the clouds, the peaks. Even now in my dreams I see my school; I see my teachers, my classrooms, the playground, the football match, the cultural evening. I read books on school education. From John Dewey to Jidu Krishnamurti—I love to swim into the ocean of pedagogic experimentations. I feel eager to meet school teachers who inspire, motivate, and arouse hope in the tender mind of the child. And on my part I encourage my students to write their dissertations and theses on the dynamics of school education. At a time when my university looks extremely intellectualized—a place where seminars after seminars, publications after publications produce only discontent, a place that celebrates the narcissism of the intellectual elite, a place that does not touch one's heart, I feel like leaving, walking through a village, entering a school, and playing with children. It is not romantic indulgence. Instead, I feel that it is important to remember that when the burden of 'knowledge' destroys the child within us, some terrible damage to our inner selves takes place. To live with children, to communicate with them, to enchant them, and to be enchanted by them—I believe—is the ultimate strength of a teacher.

Possibly from my own engagement with my daughter's education I have realized what it means to grow up with a child. I worked with her, with her books, pencils and colours. My 'scholarship' didn't matter. It didn't matter how many PhD students I had supervised. What really mattered was my patience—the ability to remain calm, despite her naughtiness, the

urge to enter her world, and become a child once again. What a great feeling it was when I saw her writing a simple sentence, and then one day a story, solving a mathematical puzzle, making a scientific experiment, reading a book, and asking questions! And at every moment of this journey I realized the beauty of this vocation: how challenging and creative it is to engage with a child, to make her understand that 1/3 is less than 1/2, that an apple falls down from the tree because of the law of gravitation. I have never felt that I am doing something dull, something intellectually inferior. Instead, I have always felt that while, because of my practice, it is not so difficult to communicate with university scholars, it is not so easy for me to engage with children. They make me humble. Once I was asked to interact with the children of Standard VIII, and initiate a discussion on Mohandas Karamchand Gandhi. I still remember my nervousness, the kind of work I did, the seriousness with which I studied Gandhi's 'experiments'. I was becoming a child, and imagining how as a child I would have found Gandhi—quite often received as an old-fashioned gentleman with strange ideas—interesting and meaningful. I thought; I reflected. I was completely engrossed. I rediscovered Gandhi—not necessarily Ashis Nandy's Gandhi, or the Gandhi of *Economic and Political Weekly*, but the Gandhi who lied, who failed, who repented, yet tried to stand up. That

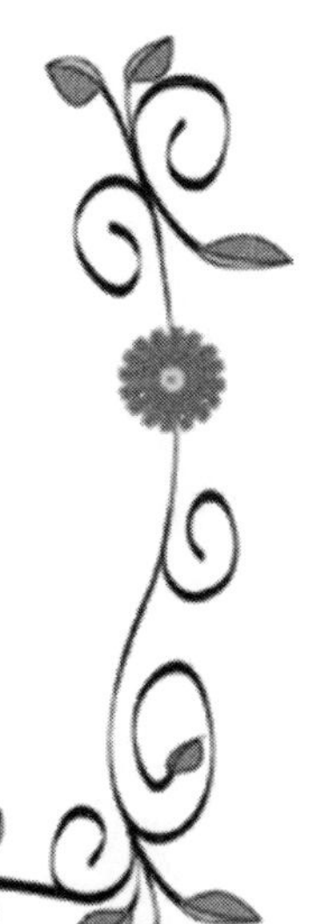

is the truth. To become a child, or, to arouse a child's interest in biography, in history, in literature is the most challenging task. Yes, I am fortunate. My experiences have enabled me to overcome the hierarchy: university vs. school, higher education vs. school education. A teacher is a teacher. No matter who her/his students are, at every stage a teacher ought to be creative and alive—intellectually, ethically, spiritually.

Now I understand why some of our finest minds gave so much attention to school education. The fate of our civilization depends on how our children grow up, how their innate possibilities are allowed to develop, how they make sense of the world, and how, despite life's long journey, they retain what they are gifted with—spontaneity, laughter, wonder, love and boundless energy. It was, therefore, not surprising that a gifted poet like Rabindranath Tagore could dare to experiment with a deeply aesthetic/ emancipatory form of education; never could the poet appreciate a typical 'schooled' consciousness that restrains the child, and dissociates her/him from a sense of the infinite prevalent in the abundance of nature. And Gandhi, despite his intense engagement in the freedom struggle, could manage to elaborate his philosophy of basic and integral education. To know about Leo Tolstoy and his experiment with education is a great feeling. Illich and Freire fascinate us. And who would like to miss Jidu Krishnamurti's revealing conversation with the children and teachers of Rishi Valley School? Great thoughts, great efforts! Yet, it is tragic that we do not take school education seriously. 'Anybody can do it. It does not require much talent or intelligence. Just manage to get a B Ed degree from any of the existing education shops, and become a school teacher!' That is the way the larger society looks at it. See its devastating consequences. Not many creative people wish to become school teachers; societal perception, poor salary, life-negating hierarchy—everything seems to prevent the growth of an appropriate ambience for school teachers. The result is that barring exceptions, they remain demotivated with a negative self-perception. The job is seen to be 'inferior'—not for the best minds! Our universities, as a result, remain dissociated from schools. Our professors, researchers and scholars love to live in their own world of 'academic excellence'; and school teachers continue to complete the syllabus imposed from above, reproduce the prescribed texts, receive the dictates of the Principal and school management, and earn some extra money through the notorious chain of private tuitions. The routine goes on. There is no creativity, no light from the world of ideas and research.

My heart aches. This duality must be broken. I feel that university professors must spend some time in teaching schoolchildren,

and working with school teachers. Apart from the dissemination of ideas, it would make them humble, enable them to regain their lost innocence, and experience once again that laughter, that spontaneity, that wonder, that naughtiness. And I believe that school teachers should be encouraged to come to the university, attend workshops, visit libraries and laboratories, and interact with researchers and professors. This would enable them to keep the flame of knowledge alive. In the ultimate analysis this constant interaction would create a brilliant community of teachers. I know that what I am imagining does not exist. Yet, I keep dreaming of this bridge. And dreams are indeed powerful; dreams inspire, shape my pedagogic practices. I teach a course on Sociology of Education. My students study Michael Apple and Pierre Bourdieu, and evolve a rigorous critique of school texts—their politics, their ideological messages, their biases. That alone is not sufficient, I tell them. I give them an assignment: 'Visit a school. Interact with the children. Explore the way they look at these texts. And then, if you are critical of the existing text, write a sample chapter—an alternative chapter—that you would want the children to read.' The assignment leads to immense dynamism. My students see beyond the university library, enter the school, rediscover their childhood; they write, intervene and contribute. 'What is the feeling?' I ask them. 'Sir, it is great. We have learned so much while writing for schoolchildren'. I keep moving. Yet, another batch, another group of students—I send them to a school, ask them to choose a group of children, interact with them and their parents. I persuade them to invite the children and their parents to our Centre. I inspire them to organize a day long workshop with them. They become sufficiently enthusiastic. They invite some university professors—a physicist, a theatre personality, a historian, a literary figure, and request them to interact with the children and their parents, and initiate a participatory discussion on education, vocation and life's multiple pursuits. The wall breaks down; university professors and schoolchildren share some golden moments.

The machine that has emerged in the name of education, I admit, is life-threatening. Sometimes I feel that the machine is destroying the child, and transforming her/him into an adult: dreamless, armoured, cynical. Is it that schools, because of reckless competition, obsession with 'success' and exam performance, and overloaded curriculum combined with the parental pressure, are writing the obituary of childhood—its wonder, its laughter, its boundless energy? I begin to look at myself. I thank God; the machine has not yet succeeded in killing the child within me. I look at my students. I pray: let the child within them remain alive; let them see the world, pass

through a spectrum of experiences; yet, let them retain their innocence, wonder and joy. The child within me begins to communicate with the child within them. True, they are serious students; they are researchers; they read thick books, write complex essays. Yet, I seek to arouse their hidden childhood. I persuade them to sing and dance, to laugh and cry, to use pencils and colours, to decorate the walls of the Centre with aesthetically designed magazines, to organize cultural programmes, to enjoy the aesthetics of food and laughter. My university becomes my school; my school becomes my university. Dear students, whisper...whisper in my ears William Blake's 'songs of innocence'. I wish to seek refuge in my mother's womb.

18

Give, my dear, give the way you breathe. Give your compassion, your love, your energy, your positive vibrations, and realize that your resources are infinite. Let education be a song of offering.

How wonderful it is to offer, to give, to flow like a fountain. What an extraordinary feeling it is when one melts, loves, shares, gives oneself. These are the moments when one feels that one's true richness lies in the act of becoming empty—the act of sharing, not possessing; the act of giving, not holding. To possess or to accumulate is to remain in an eternal trap of fear and anxiety leading to the poverty of consciousness. Yet, how sad it is that this simple truth is seldom realized in our educational enterprise! Instead, we have been told—and told repeatedly by our parents, teachers and the larger society—that if you are educated you invariably acquire the right to possess, to accumulate, to gain extra privileges. The more educated you are the more privileged you are. You gain a 'position'; your 'status' is your ability to differentiate yourself from others; you are supposed to be ambitious, rich and powerful. It is, therefore, not surprising that all the time we are talking about our rights, our privileges, our salaries. Professors are measuring their 'intelligence'—you get a project, a lucrative one, and hence your department room must have an AC! Or, for that matter, a student thinks that her success must be measured in terms of her placement—the package she receives. The entire discourse, it seems, is centred on the principle of having and possessing. And it is sanctified through a culture of learning that has already conditioned our minds.

I am not different. I have become an integral component of this culture. How much have I gained? What have I got? Should I get more? These questions confront me, and paradoxically I realize that the more I raise these questions the more mean, anxiety-ridden and insecure I become. I realize that I am in a trap. The more I get, the more I demand; the more I seek to possess, the more poverty-stricken I become in my consciousness. Because poverty is not just an economic index; poverty is also a state of consciousness. I keep desiring and desiring. I become a beggar. I can't share. I can't offer. I can't give. There is fear; there is fear that if I give, if I share, I would lose. I fail to realize that only when I give I become truly rich. Is it that universities are making us neurotically restless? We are becoming discontented—living with fear, psychic poverty and chronic anxiety.

Yet, there are moments when I realize the cost of this pathology. And then comes the saner moments—the moments of deep contemplation. I look at the sun; I realize that it is giving me life, warmth and energy. I look at the moon; I realize that it gives me the aesthetics of beauty, the sublime light of illumination. I approach a tree; it gives me its shade, its perseverance, its companionship. I see a flower; it gives me its fragrance. I see a bird in the blue sky; it gives me the beauty of imagination, the urge to touch the sky. Mountains, rivers, oceans—they all give me. And I realize that in the act of giving nature is truly rich; its abundance is its beauty; it doesn't hold, it flows; it doesn't possess, it offers. And then I pray: let nature be my guru, my ultimate tutor. Something happens. There is calmness. Fear tends to wither away. Every act of ours, I tell myself, should emanate from the principle of giving. It is sad that our schools, colleges and universities have lost this rhythmic connectedness with nature. Our science 'conquers' nature; our closed classrooms dissociate ourselves from the infinite space that nature provides; our burden of knowledge makes us incapable of becoming sufficiently light to fly; our ego-boosting exercise through the rituals of seminars and placement cells makes us forget that life is not just about possessing, it is essentially about giving.

However, I rise. I feel inspired to narrate yet another possibility, another story of

education. As a teacher I ask myself: What is teaching? Thank God, I find an answer—an answer that makes me calm. Teaching is nothing but an act of giving, sharing, offering. True, it is a job; I receive a decent salary; the university gives me comfortable accommodation. Possibly I receive more than I deserve. Yet, there is something in the vocation of teaching that takes it beyond the logic of calculation. The art of teaching emanates from the urge to share. A teacher's ultimate fulfilment lies in the act of giving everything that he has—ideas, thoughts, realizations, discoveries, interpretations, facts, theories, and above all the flow of life-energy. And in that act of giving a teacher finds everything: love, clarity, wisdom. Dualities disappear; fear vanishes; giving becomes receiving. And what about studentship? Is it possible to bloom without giving, without offering oneself? But what does one give? No, it is not a question of money. In fact, the act of giving becomes deeply meaningful when one gives one's fragrance, one's positivity, one's concern, one's humanity, one's realization that at a deeper level one is inseparable from others. It is in this sense that to give is not the privilege of only those who are materially rich and wealthy. Quote often, that 'richness' itself might prove to be an obstacle to the art of giving. That is why, dear students, I seek to tell you: you can give only when you realize that to love is to give. How wonderful it would have been had our studentship been filled with this principle of giving! As I see our campus, I see that our students with their hyper- political sensibilities are conscious of their rights. They are demanding, demanding all the time because as modern political citizens they are concerned about their rights. They demand fellowships; they demand new hostels; they demand transparency in the admission process. Granted, these demands have their legitimacy. Yet, seldom does one see a similar concern with the ethos of giving. Imagine how the culture of the university would have changed had they given their love to the natural landscape, reduced their dependence on motor cycles, planted and protected trees, and created an environment conducive to bio-diversity. Imagine what would have happened had our students opened a night school for those young boys working day and night at our *dhabas*. Imagine what a difference it would have made to the vibrations of our university had our students visited a neighbouring MCD school and offered a beautiful gift—their passion for books and ideas—to the children. Or, for that matter, imagine what would have happened had we—university professors—minimized the use of costly cars for coming to the department, reduced our dependence on ACs and other electronic appliances to create a more eco-sensitive campus. How graceful it would have been had we all planted and nurtured trees,

instead of demolishing these for creating a parking space for our ever growing cars and bikes. I am aware that these simple acts or gestures may not seem like sufficiently political or radical or even intellectually stimulating to charm the academic community. But then, how do we forget that to create is to love, and it is always simple and unassuming?

The ethos of giving/offering I am talking about is not charity. Because charity means the celebration of the inflated ego of the giver; it is like asserting: 'I am privileged. I am rich. And you need my sympathy. I am protecting you.' In fact, in charity one does not really give; instead, the ego gets inflated; one acquires a 'name'. It humiliates the receiver; the receiver is objectified. It fails to realize that we are all givers and receivers at the same time. As a matter of fact, in my offering I receive my ultimate treasure. That is why, the ethos of giving I am talking about is not a separate act; it is as normal as breathing; it is not conscious of itself. It is one's being, one's rhythm, one's existence. An awakening of the naturalness of giving is what education ought to be. It is sad that education has become unnatural. And hence the enterprise of giving is seen as a separate/specialized act which the academic establishment regards as 'social work'—a professional course that trains and manufactures 'social workers' for NGOs. While 'social work' as a specialized course may have its meanings, I am suggesting something else. I am suggesting that to offer, to give, to serve one need not hold a degree; let it be a natural process. Let the spirit of giving characterize every aspect of one's being.

It is at this juncture that I recall an incident. I have asked my students to visit a series of old age homes, interview the inmates, and write their life-histories. Yes, it is an exercise which, academically speaking, is very important for the students doing a course on Methods of Social Sciences. Yet, despite this technical task, something happens. It becomes difficult for some of my students to just interview the inmates. They get involved; and the relationship no longer remains that of a 'researcher-respondent' relationship. My students begin to offer—naturally, spontaneously. What do they offer? No, not money. But they offer their concern, their smiles, their tales, their touch, their vibrations, their prayer. And as I see, my students become richer. Because in that act of giving they receive something special; they receive the feeling that they are not just technical people; they have a heart that aches, that loves. With tears and pain, with love and prayer, with ambiguities (I am a researcher; I can't stay with them forever; yet, I can't remain aloof) and existential questions relating to old age and life's inexplicable suffering they grow, they rediscover themselves. And I learn a lesson. We must alter the dominant notion of 'field work'

in which we are primarily interested in taking and accumulating facts, information and interviews for our research publications. It is instrumental. Is it possible to bring the ethic of care into the domain of our field work? I believe it is. Only then does research becomes an act of offering.

True, we live in an unnatural world. What is simple and profound is forgotten. Instead of the ethos of giving, the urge to receive becomes important. And that leads to all that we see in our times: exploitation, poverty, violence, injustice, war. Dear students, believe it: Marx's 'class conflict' exists because there is no giving, there is only an urge to hoard, accumulate and exploit; Simone de Beauvoir's 'patriarchy' prevails because men have forgotten to love and surrender, they know only possession—possession of women as their private property; Foucault's 'surveillance' machinery functions because power has become the power to hierarchize and normalize, and we have forgotten to realize the beauty of the power to be powerless. And hence don't just theorize. Live, and what else is living except the art of giving, the art that makes one abundant and profound? Give, my dear, give the way you breathe. Give your compassion, your love, your energy, your positive vibrations, and realize that your inner resources are infinite. Let education be a song of offering.

19

I have no 'original' idea; I am incapable of revolutionizing human thought. I know that this temporal existence of mine will be forgotten as soon as I die. There is no reason to believe that as a teacher or a writer, my words have an impact on anybody....I exist for some time. I enjoy. But then, I will be forgotten; I will be reduced into zero. That is the reality. Everything else is an illusion.

The other day a young Associate Professor from a leading university in the capital came to see me. Her academic brilliance was quite visible and evident. Yet, I felt some sort of anger and restlessness in her persona. 'Is everyone in the department equally serious? Are they writing anything substantial? Or, are they just producing papers which virtually have no *impact factor*?' She kept alleging and comparing; and this preoccupation with what academicians are fond of regarding as 'impact factor', I felt, seems to have generated a lot of negativity in her being. It seems that it is no longer possible for her to work with joy and ease—without comparing, without measuring, without thinking how bad others are, and how good she is. 'Maybe I haven't published much. But whatever I have done has got tremendous impact factor,' she reminded me. She, I felt, must have done commendable work, and written something which her discipline regards as substantial. Yet, there was no positivity, no contentment, no joy. In her pride there was anger; in her assertion there was a scale for measurement. It was not graceful. What would have happened to her, had there been no impact factor? Would she stop writing, creating, thinking? I kept asking myself.

I made her a cup of tea. In order to lighten the ambience I started talking about politics, cricket, the weather and television serials. But academicians are pretty serious people. They do not smile easily. She left. But then, I started thinking about the much discussed 'impact factor'. What sort of 'impact' are we talking about? You write a paper. And I quote you in the paper I write. Or, I include your book in the bibliography of the book I write. And more and more scholars do so. It satisfies you. You feel that your writing has been taken seriously, and you have acquired a 'name' in the field. In other words, you are having an impact! The game goes on—the game of quotes, references, citation index, journals with good 'impact factor', and the intoxication with measurement —almost like the number of centuries cricket commentators calculate when they talk about Sachin Tendulkar. And this causes restlessness. The worth of everything that you do has to be seen in terms of this scale. No matter how paradoxical it may sound, the fact is that in the process you lose confidence and faith in yourself because if others do not refer to your work, you feel yourself worthless. And in a not so innocent world there is also the politics of who quotes whom, who neglects whom, who gives awards to whom. And once you fall into this trap you lose the grace that a truly gifted thinker or a reflexive mind needs; you lose calmness, humility, the eternal smile—the ability to laugh at yourself.

And then I begin to locate myself in this culture of high academics. Do I have an impact? I ask myself. 'No, not at all,' I assure myself. My emptiness gives me immense freedom. I write what I feel I should write. I value my inner voice, my own rhythm rather than the 'impact factor' of the journals. I do not know whether I am being quoted or not; but what I know is that I am ordinary and temporal, and I need not take myself so seriously; like the tides in the ocean people like me are coming and disappearing. The only thing I can do is to act with this clarity, and celebrate it without pretention, without arrogance. And hence I write not out of compulsion (see the way the pressure operates—you must write, otherwise what would your colleagues think about you), not because I have to prove something (see the way they whisper in your ears—you are nothing if you are not sought after at seminars, conferences and selection committees); I write when my heart embraces my brain, and there is a dance in my entire being. True, I have no

'original' idea; I am incapable of revolutionizing human thought. I know that this temporal existence of mine will be forgotten as soon as I die. There is no reason to believe that as a teacher or a writer, my words have an impact on anybody. But I have some wonder, some curiosity, some urge to communicate my experiences, my ways of seeing, rediscovering culture, life and politics; and that leads me to write—not so frequently, but occasionally—on modernity, on education, on culture, on religiosity. I am sure there is no 'impact'. However, if there are moments when someone writes an encouraging review, sends a letter, conveys a message that she/he has been touched by my writings or teaching, I feel that it is something extra, it is my bonus. But my work does not depend on whether or not it has its 'impact'—the way in the early hours of the morning I come to the balcony, and wait eagerly for the sunrise without bothering whether my communion with this miracle does have an impact on the economy of the nation. I exist for some time. I enjoy. But then, I will be forgotten; I will be reduced into zero. That is the reality. Everything else is an illusion.

My enquiry doesn't stop. I know that I don't have an impact. But what is it that has had an impact on me? I ask myself. Yes, I am a professor. I teach. My students write their dissertations and theses. I read books, research papers, and mention these in lectures and

seminars. But is it really true that these writings—even if as a professional sociologist, as a supervisor I am required to mention these—have a genuine impact on me—the way I think, see the world, make sense of my life? I don't think so. Yes, if I teach a course in Social Stratification, I will mention all sorts of writings on caste produced by some of our celebrity sociologists; but, frankly speaking, as I see myself, most of these have no impact on me. I am not touched. My heart does not ache; tears do not flow; there is no inspiration to create a better world. And given a chance, I would not read these works for the second time; I would not like to touch, smell and keep these books in my bed. But no matter where I am, I would love to read Premchand's short stories to feel the pathology of caste; I would like to know more and more about Gandhi's experiments for overcoming the hierarchy of caste; or a gardener with the so-called 'low caste' origin nurturing flowers that would bring the likes of Blake and Wordsworth closer to him would make me see the absurdity of the casteist division between the mental and the manual. The paradox is that the scholars I refer to in my lectures, and occasionally in my bibliography (because of a purely professional reason) need not necessarily have a powerful impact on me. Possibly I do not fit into the model academic box. Because I do not divorce my head from my heart, my science from my poetry, my academics from my

life, my discourses from my tears. For example, if someone tells me: 'You are intelligent. You are a scholar. You have read so much', I do not feel very happy. Instead, if someone says: 'What you have said or written has made me feel. It has touched me. I have shared it with my mother, my friend, my beloved', I feel God is blessing me. Likewise, I am not touched by the mere 'intelligence' of a scholar; nor am I touched by his/her academic profile—how many books, papers, prizes.... What influences me is one's ability to touch my entire being. To take yet another illustration, these days in the arena of higher academics, we see the proliferation of scholars in the field of 'cultural studies'; they, as it is said, are highly valued; with their publications in all sorts of trendy journals, they must have a huge 'impact factor'; but they have no impact on me, because most of the time I do not understand them, I do not understand their complex prose, their references, their vocabulary. However, a film by Ray (what an extraordinary poetry on celluloid!), or say, an autobiography of Kamala Das (written with great lucidity and honesty) does have a tremendous impact on me, on my modes of understanding meaningful cinema, or the location of women in a patriarchal society. It enriches my sensitivity to culture, aesthetics and gender.

One may allege that I am deviating; I am denying the logic of the academic discipline; I

am emphasizing spiritual/aesthetic influences rather than the 'academic' impact. I need not defend myself. Yet, I can say that I am dealing with the domain of human sciences; I am not talking about mathematics or physics; and how is it possible to enter the domain of human sciences without referring to aesthetics, poetry and spirituality? I learn about the way human societies function not just through the pages of *The Contributions to Indian Sociology*, or *Economic and Political Weekly*, I learn through literature and philosophy, through films and music, through biographies and reflexive writings. And is it necessary that I have to be necessarily influenced by professional sociologists and their publications? I don't think so. As I have already indicated, disembodied/heavily reference-oriented prose, statistics, theoretical complexity and the density of loaded words alone are not sufficient to have an impact on me. Maybe something very simple and yet immensely profound—say, a poem by Muktibodh, an Upanishadic prayer, a short story by Saadat Hasan Manto—influences me more than these academic writings. This is not to suggest that nobody from the academic world has made an impact on me. I have survived because even today I love to read Karl Marx's *Economic and Philosophic Manuscripts of 1844*; my romance with Erich Fromm and Herbert Marcuse has not stopped; Max Weber's reflections on 'science as a vocation' make me think; I feel like going back

to Emile Durkheim's penetrating insights into symbolism in the study of the 'elementary forms of religious life'; Ashis Nandy's notes on the 'intimate enemy' in the context of our colonial history have charmed me; and yes, there are many more examples. But then, most of the publications we are compelled to quote and refer (what else can you do because your professors ask you to write a lengthy review of literature in your theses, or the journals/ publication houses demand that you must quote a particular kind of texts?) do not have much impact on me. I am well aware of the fact that my liking/disliking does not mean anything in the way the academic world looks at itself. But at the same time I am sufficiently free to reclaim my space, and say that I need not be always influenced by their criterion of 'impact factor'.

Meanwhile, I ask myself strange questions. Did Jesus Christ or Gautam Buddha have an 'impact factor'? True, they influenced us, and influenced us deeply. Yet, at one level nothing seems to have changed. We do not love our neighbours; we cause war; the Sermon on the Mount is almost forgotten. We do not strive for *nirvana*; we find ourselves trapped into the cycle of *samsara*; instead of the four 'noble truths', we live in a jungle of lies. Where is then the lasting impact? Intellectual cognition is one thing; and the real impact on the life we lead is quite another. But see the irony. We academicians,

because of some publications in trendy journals, begin to think that we have a great impact (what sort of impact it is?) Is it ignorance? Or, is it the culture of narcissism? Or, is it a very shallow notion of impact—merely intellectual impact, but no impact on the *dharma* of everyday life? I find no easy answer. Meanwhile, the mountains call me. The radiant sun sends its divine message to the snowy peaks. I become a witness. I forget the grammar of citation index and impact factor; I realize the superficiality of the game of publications because I see the most beautiful book unfolding itself before my own eyes. No dispute any more; it is the moment of silence.

20

I realize that it is difficult to exist as just a 'supervisor'; a relationship is established—a relationship that transcends the boundaries of statistics, empiricism, ethnography, review of literature and post-PhD publications. I do not wish to eradicate or deny this tension because, I believe, a teacher lives in many domains simultaneously.

I was a research scholar pursuing my doctoral work; and my father used to remind me: 'You should always remain polite, and whenever there is a crisis in life consult your 'guide', and do whatever he suggests.' He was not from the world of academics; he was not used to the idea of a 'supervisor' as a mere subject specialist; for him, unlike many of us who assert the need for a hard core professional relationship between the teacher and the taught, a guide was not just a supervisor; a guide, he felt, should be like Krishna taking his disciple Arjuna to a higher level of realization. His task, my father must have thought, was more than just instructing his student how to collect data, how to theorize, how to arrange chapters, and write a thesis to which the external examiner would find no reason to object; a guide, for him, should be a philosopher, a counsellor, a true friend.

And today I find myself in a new situation.

I am no longer a research scholar; instead, I teach, and research scholars work with me. Who am I? Am I a 'guide' in the way my father visualized it? Or, am I just a 'supervisor'—a subject specialist concerned only with the academic life of the student? These questions haunt me; and I find no easy answer. True, I know my limitations; I don't have the wisdom that my father thought a 'guide' ought to have. But at the same time I realize that it is difficult to exist as just a 'supervisor'; a relationship is established—a relationship that transcends the boundaries of statistics, empiricism, ethnography, review of literature and post-PhD publications. I do not wish to eradicate or deny this tension because, I believe, a teacher lives in many domains simultaneously.

To begin with, let me ask myself a pertinent question: Am I a true researcher capable of supervising my M Phil/PhD students? I am not very sure. I love to see myself primarily as a teacher, not a researcher. Yes, I am aware of the fact that good teaching involves a fair degree of familiarity with the latest research trends, and a good researcher can also be a great teacher. However, I cannot imagine myself engaging only in research and publications; my *swadharma*, I feel, is that of a teacher engaging in an act of communion with students. And, therefore, I have no hesitation to say that I am not a very solid researcher—a researcher who is excessively focused, specialized, and a master of a tiny domain of enquiry. I move; I fly; I transcend boundaries; literature, sociology, metaphysics—everything attracts; and as a result, life itself—modernity, culture, education, social theory—becomes my area of interest. It is this passion—not necessarily a very focused/specialized knowledge—that makes me communicate with my research students. I do not know whether as a supervisor I am of any help to them. However, there is only one thing I can do. My passion inspires me; ideas strike my imagination; I share those ideas with my students; and as a result, something happens. They too get inspired, and find a theme for further research. I remember my first M Phil student. He was a young man with a political dream. He read Marx; but he was not a conventional Marxist. And then one day I asked him to study Erich Fromm's *The Sane Society*. He read; he was excited; and then, I whispered in his ears: 'You can write an M Phil dissertation on Erich Fromm's notion of freedom.' He got it, and wrote a reasonably good dissertation. It was his work. I am sure there were more equipped professors in the department to tell him about Erich Fromm: his critical engagement with Sigmund Freud and Karl Marx, his plea for humanistic psychoanalysis, his critique of authoritarianism, his dissenting voice against the culture of consumption, and his quest for the art of loving. In that sense I didn't help him much. But I only acted as a catalyst. Nothing

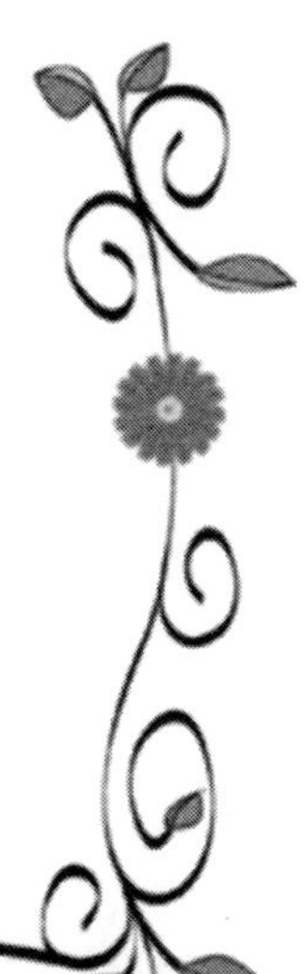

more. Nothing less. Time passed. And again, to take yet another example, a young man arrived who was not very sure about his research area. My engagement with him began; and slowly I realized that he was deeply religious; and his interest in the ashram life was truly remarkable. I suggested to him: 'Choose an ashram, do a rigorous ethnography of the ashram, see its notion of time, space, food, prayer and speech, and write a thesis on the ashram as a site for alternative culture.' I saw light in his face. 'Sir, now I have got the topic. For me, it is not just the academic question; it is my life's quest.' And he came forward with a reasonably meaningful thesis. True, I didn't know anything about the ashram he studied; nor did I know much about the particular religious sect he was referring to. He could have got a better supervisor specialized in the field of the sociology of religion. My only satisfaction was that I could become a companion in his search for a research enquiry.

I know my limitations. I am not a researcher. I am a teacher. Never did I try to hide this fact from my students. Yet, I am fortunate; many bright students have come forward and worked with me; and as a result, I have grown, and learned immensely from them. Their interests were diverse and many; my horizon kept expanding. How wonderful it is to recall those days—an Iranian student reading his chapters on the intellectual traditions in post-Ayotollah

Khomeni Iran, and I am listening with great care, learning and at the same time suggesting some possibilities to further improve the thesis; a student sharing his field notes collected from the Hindi film industry, and we are engaged in a discussion on the changing notion of 'masculinity' in our Hindi films, and this act of mutual learning inspiring my student to write an innovative thesis; a student writing about Allama Iqbal, his poetry and politics, and I am continually moving from one world to another—from Tagore to Iqbal, from Iqbal to Tagore. In a way, my research students become my young tutors, and I enjoy this experience. The story goes on. One writes an M Phil dissertation on partition violence and Saadat Hasan Manto's writings; my literary sensibilities develop; Manto enters my inner world. Or for that matter, when an Assamese student chooses to write her dissertation on Bhupen Hazarika and the sociology of music, I grow and learn many details about the great singer which I didn't know earlier. True, my age, my experience might have helped me to give some kind of coherence and direction to their dissertations and theses. But how can I deny that they have enabled me to grow and evolve with them? Possibly I am not a supervisor. I am more like a wanderer, a co-traveller.

And in the process something happened. I ceased to exist as just a 'supervisor'—an expert

who directs and only talks about chapters, references, logical coherence and argumentation. No, as I have already said, I do not have the wisdom to become the kind of 'guide' that my father idealized. However, I found myself in a fluid zone. We could not make a clear demarcation between the thesis and the curve of human life; and as a result, many of my research students took me to a world beyond footnotes, methods and theories. A student of mine wrote a good dissertation on culture and gender. There was a promise in her work; and I suggested to her a tentative PhD theme on feminism and women ascetics. She was prepared and enthusiastic. And then she became a mother; her child, needless to add, became her book, her thesis; it was becoming increasingly difficult for her to continue her university life. 'What should I do, Sir? I know that home is not everything for a woman; all my friends are writing their theses. But Sir, I feel guilty if I do not give adequate attention to my child. At this stage God wants me to be with my child. Sir, what do you think?' she asked me. I could not say: 'Why are you bothering me? It is your personal problem. I am here only to look at your chapters.' Instead, I listened, listened with great care, and then one day I suggested to her: 'For the time being you can withdraw and de-register yourself from the university because at this juncture you need to fulfil yourself as a mother, and it is this life-affirming experience that will enrich you immensely. You will miss nothing. Instead, when after a couple years you come back, your entry into the discourse of feminism is likely to acquire a new meaning.' She gave her consent. Who was I at that moment—a 'supervisor', a subject specialist, a 'guide', or a concerned friend who empathizes, who listens? The journey with research students has its ups and downs; and I too realize that I cannot exist as merely an 'expert'; I enter into the domain of life—its moments of glory and its moments of pain and disorder. 'Sir, I have to consult a psychiatrist. For quite some time I am not in a position to concentrate. Sorry Sir, I can't show you my work', a student expressed her utter helplessness. 'Don't worry. Tell me what has happened to you?' I sought to assure her. 'I don't know, Sir. I find no inspiration, no meaning in what I am doing. Moreover, I can't escape the trap of anxiety. What will happen to me? Can I take care of myself, of my old parents?' I forgot her research plan; I began to walk with her. And the dialogue continued. I don't know whether our conversation really helped her to find herself—her innate potential, her ability to find joy and meaning in simple and profound things of life, her eternal spirit that knows that anxiety takes us nowhere because the next moment is unknown, and hence what makes sense is to live this very moment, and live intensely. But I know that

God whispered in my ears: 'It is not easy, my dear, to become a guide. It is a long journey.'

Meanwhile, my students keep writing and submitting their dissertations and theses. And I continue to learn—a young researcher tells me that the changing dynamics of the relationship between the two major religious communities can be seen in the streets of Kolkata; the phenomenal growth of play schools in the city makes a student of mine think, and she relates it to the sociology of urban/middle class living; and to take yet another example, a bright researcher keeps informing me of the new readings on Mohandas Karamchand Gandhi—his presence (even presence in absence) in diverse social movements. And at this juncture an external examiner returns the PhD thesis of one of my students. The examiner wants her to revise her thesis. She falls down; she becomes upset; she is angry; and she tells me: 'I am giving up, Sir. I have an ideological position; the examiner has not understood it. To revise the thesis is to go against my conviction.' I sit with her; I try to make her calm; I want her to see that there is nothing unusual if the examiner asks a researcher to make some revisions; and there is no harm if she does it; and with more maturity and hard work she can always sharpen her arguments and eventually publish her work. She passes through emotional turmoil. I play a role—a minimal role—in making her rise once again. In the process, I do not know when

I have ceased to become a mere supervisor. But who am I? I look at the sky, and ask myself how many times I have to be born in this world in order to come closer to my father's visualization of a true 'guide'.